WILDERNESS
CHEF

DEDICATION

For Kristian

Son, you once gave me a book of blank pages to fill with my favourite recipes for you. That was the inspiration for this book. I hope you do not mind that I have shared these recipes with a slightly larger audience.

Much love,
Dad

CONWAY
Bloomsbury Publishing Plc
50 Bedford Square, London, WC1B 3DP, UK

BLOOMSBURY, CONWAY and the Conway logo are trademarks of Bloomsbury Publishing Plc

First published in 2020

A catalogue record for this book is available from the British Library

Library of Congress Cataloguing-in-Publication data has been applied for

ISBN: 978-1-8448-6582-6; ePub: 978-1-8448-6583-3; ePDF: 978-1-8448-6581-9

10 9 8 7 6 5 4 3 2 1

Designed by Austin Taylor
Typeset in Swift Leicht and Renos Rough
Printed and bound in China by Toppan Leefung Printing

Bloomsbury Publishing Plc makes every effort to ensure that the papers used in the manufacture of our books are natural, recyclable products made from wood grown in well-managed forests. Our manufacturing processes conform to the environmental regulations of the country of origin.

To find out more about our authors and books visit www.bloomsbury.com and sign up for our newsletters.

WILDERNESS
CHEF

THE ULTIMATE GUIDE TO
COOKING OUTDOORS

RAY MEARS

CONWAY
LONDON · OXFORD · NEW YORK · NEW DELHI · SYDNEY

CONTENTS

ABOUT THE AUTHOR

RAY MEARS is recognised throughout the world as a genuine authority on the subjects of bushcraft, tracking and survival skills. For nearly forty years he has worked to communicate his passion for his subject, connecting people more closely with nature through Woodlore, his school of wilderness bushcraft.

Ray has also become a household name through his writing and television series, including *Tracks, World of Survival, Trips Money Can't Buy* with Ewan McGregor, *The Real Heroes of Telemark* and many more. These programmes have reached out and touched the hearts of everyone, from small children to grandparents. They are enjoyed by many because of Ray's down to earth approach, his obvious love for his subject and the empathy and respect he shows for indigenous peoples and their cultures. Ray has spent his life learning these skills and is truly a master of the subject he calls *Wilderness Bushcraft*.

For Ray, cookery in the wild means more than simply providing hearty and sustaining nourishment; it is also a means to bolster morale in times of difficulty. If you could accompany him on a journey into the wild and witness his passion for wild foods – be they the treasure of wild mushrooms, the fragrance of wild herbs, or a trout caught with hook, line and native cunning – you might discover something more; for Ray cooking is a deeply spiritual process, an honouring and celebration of the ingredients provided by the land, the lake and the stream.

OTHER BOOKS BY RAY MEARS

Out on the Land: Bushcraft Skills from the Northern Forest

Bushcraft

Bushcraft Survival

Essential Bushcraft

Northern Wilderness

Outdoor Survival Handbook: A Guide to the Resources and Materials Available in the Wild and How to Use Them for Food, Shelter, Warmth And Navigation

My Outdoor Life

The Real Heroes of Telemark: The True Story of the Secret Mission to Stop Hitler's Atomic Bomb

The Survival Handbook

Ray Mears Goes Walkabout

Ray Mears' World of Survival

Vanishing World: A Life of Bushcraft

Wild Food

INTRODUCTION

IT WAS MY FIRST DAY WITH THE SANEMA TRIBE, deep in the pristine rainforest at the head of the Orinoco River, Venezuela. The decision had been made to hike out and recce an outlying village. I had no idea how far this would be, only that it would be a full day's walking, and that I would be staying there the night and returning the following day.

Rainforest Indians are strong walkers with sinews adapted to the tough conditions of their country. I stripped my pack to the absolute bare essentials to lighten my load. My two guides were equipped with machetes and basket packs carried on tumplines across their foreheads; one sported a hat fashioned from the scalp of the sloth, giving him the incongruous look of a 1970s bewigged game-show host. One carried a blowpipe and poison darts, the other an ancient side-by-side shotgun scarlet with rust.

I was determined to keep up with my guides so as to make a good impression for the coming days. Unsurprisingly, the walk was arduous, sliding down muddy precipices, fording streams and climbing up steep ridges. Keeping pace with the guides was as difficult as I had imagined; apart from an occasional halt, the most I saw of them were the still-moving leaves of the undergrowth ahead, indicating that they had just passed.

At about midday, we ascended a steep slope. Clambering over fallen rainforest giants, I found myself cresting and then descending a long, gently sloping ridge. Suddenly, I heard the pop of the shotgun being fired somewhere ahead. Now, as I continued down the slope, I saw feathers on the ground; one of the guides had clearly shot a bird and was plucking it as he walked. The trail steepened and came down to a tiny stream. Here, the guides – I am glad to say looking as fatigued as I felt – had stopped and were squatting by a small fire they had kindled. As I took off my pack, I noticed the hunter take the bird he had plucked. He picked a nearby fishtail palm leaf within which he neatly folded the bird, securing the package with the leaf midrib. This he then pushed into the embers of the fire to cook. How beautifully simple and immediate: a few minutes later the meal was complete, the small fowl steamed perfectly in its own juices. I would see

opposite Aerial view of the Orinoco River, Venezuela.

the same thing repeated again over the coming days and witness the extraordinary skill of these forest people, mimicking the call of birds to coax them into range of their deadly blowpipes.

Today, these are but distant memories, but the inspiration of such experiences never fades, nor are they unique. I have had the fortunate opportunity to travel with tribal peoples across our planet and time and again I have learned to cook a meal in the simplest of ways, utilising just sharpened sticks, leaves, moss or bark. On the west coast of North America, the tribal communities sometimes also cook underground, but each family has their own method for such cooking, their own ground oven recipe. Part of the brilliance of these methods is their simple, expedient immediacy; another part is the joy of using natural materials that will simply be

comfort of sleep, the new day will be greeted with fresh enthusiasm.

But rather than just leaving these techniques in the realm of pure survival, you can bring them into more 'civilised' situations, such as a fixed camp, where there is often scope for making more elaborate food. Just because we are living outdoors does not mean that our food need only be an insipid, pre-packaged, dehydrated 'Spag Bol'. With a little forethought and imagination, we can feast like kings outdoors. The secret lies in searching for good ingredients; ingredients that inspire culinary excellence and experimentation. These should wherever possible be locally sourced and organic, and reflect perfectly the landscape in which you find yourself – a concept so well captured in the French term *terroir*. As I hope you will discover,

> Part of the brilliance of these methods is their simple, expedient immediacy; another part is the joy of using natural materials that will simply be reabsorbed by the environment that provided them, unlike plastics or aluminium foil.

reabsorbed by the environment that provided them, unlike plastics or aluminium foil.

In the pages that follow, you will find many recipes for outdoor cooking that hark back to an aboriginal past. I have also included more safari-style cooking and advice for lightweight hiking meals. Having spent much of my life on expedition in remote places, I can say from experience that food and how it is cooked is one of the most important aspects of morale. Have a bad day, hampered by disappointment, setback and failure, and gloom seeps into the camp. But serve a tasty, exciting meal and the impossible becomes possible again, spirits rise and with the

outdoor cooking is fun and can in fact become part of your inspiration when choosing locations for outdoors adventures as you search for culinary gems to add to your list of ingredients.

Incidentally, when I finished the hike with my Sanema guides they turned to me and told me that they were tired and footsore and complained that I walked really fast. It turned out that they had decided to impress me by walking so fast that I could not catch up with them, so for the two days, in our eagerness to impress each other, we had been accelerating. We laughed, and then went in search of a hearty meal of spit-roasted capybara.

THE OUTDOOR KITCHEN

TO WATCH AN AUSTRALIAN ABORIGINAL COOKING a freshly caught goanna lizard is to witness the application of the most important lesson of outdoor cookery: keep things simple. A fire is lit, and it is arranged to provide the required heat, with enough suitable wood piled on to provide the necessary longevity. Sometimes, broken chunks of termite mound are added to give longer-lasting coals. While the fire burns towards the perfect condition for cooking, the cook sits to one side, undisturbed by the children, who have learned not to interfere, but to watch and learn as the food is prepared according to ancient tradition: cleaned and dressed with nothing more than a crudely sharpened stick. While this may seem primitive to modern eyes, this practice honours the wisdom of 'the ancestors': to cook food fresh and to eat it immediately – a mantra that ensures the food is both safe and nutrient-rich.

At its simplest, the outdoor kitchen can be the lee of a mountain boulder; at its most elaborate, a full-blown safari kitchen tent. Whatever the circumstance, successful cooking will result from more than just good ingredients; as every professional chef knows, it is not just about culinary flair. More essential still is planning, good organisation and attention to timings. Nowhere is this more true than when cooking outdoors, where we have no easy access to work surfaces or running water, there is scant refrigeration and our source of heat must be constantly attended to, be it a camping stove or a wood fire. A professional chef who once cooked outdoors with me described the whole process rather well as: 'working a lunch service while keeping twenty plates spinning'.

Whether the catering is simple or complicated, organisation is the key. This begins long before departure, when the menu is being planned. Account must be taken of the team members' dietary requirements,

KEEP IT SIMPLE

Unless we are outdoors to cook a feast, the purpose of the kitchen is to support our other activities, not to dominate them. Over-complication will lead to delays and poorly cooked meals. The well-run outdoor kitchen will support the expeditions' activities and should pass without notice. The wise chef keeps an eye on the weather and the activities being undertaken, producing more filling meals in periods of bad weather or when activities have been arduous. Lighter meals are more appropriate when days are calmer. By contrast, the badly run kitchen becomes a debilitating irritation.

the availability or lack of fresh food at the destination, the storage facilities and the style of travel we shall be engaged in. Compromise is the magic word as we balance the space and weight restrictions with our culinary aspirations.

FIXED CAMP

The fixed camp kitchen is the gold standard of outdoor cooking. Here, we usually have a dedicated kitchen tarp (tarpaulin), table and cooking fire. I prefer two fires: one to cook over and another used solely for the production of hot water for washing. In the fixed camp kitchen, I keep the catering supplies securely stored in boxes. The camp rations are stored in suitable boxes in the stores tent. In the kitchen, use three boxes: the day box, the larder box and the chef's box.

THE
DAY BOX

The day box contains the rations necessary for cooking the day's meals.

THE
LARDER
BOX

The larder box contains equipment and many smaller labelled boxes containing essential ingredients, such as flour, spices, salt, sugar and so forth. Here, practical quantities are kept on hand.

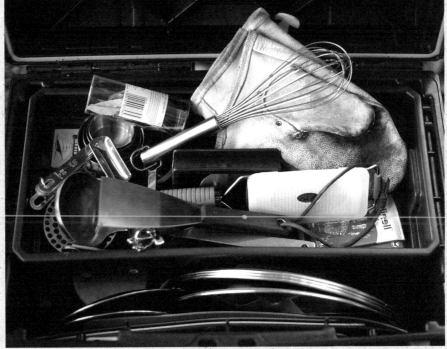

THE CHEF'S BOX

The chef's box contains the cooking
knives, apparatus and essential tools.
Kitchen knives and basic tools travel
in a canvas tool roll, which can
be hung up during cooking on
a suspended rail or taut line.

REFRIGERATOR

Even in the remotest places it
is possible to transport a camp
freezer or refrigerator in the
back of a 4x4. Today, these are
sturdy, well made and greatly
increase the scope of culinary
supplies that can be brought
along. However, they are bulky
and occupy a great deal of
space that could be utilised for
other ingredients or purposes.
They must also be properly
managed for food safety;
failure to do so can ruin a trip.

CANOE CAMP

Wilderness canoeing is a wonderful activity but is akin to spending all day in the gym. Consequently, the calorific demands are high, and meals need to be filling, tasty and quick to cook at the end of a tiring day. Fresh food can be carried for a few days, depending on the food type. For example, meat for the first day and cheese and tortilla wraps for a week or more, depending on the temperature. However, for the most part, we rely on dried and canned foodstuffs.

CANNED FOODS

Canned foods are heavy but easily transported by canoe since we only need to bodily carry our food across portage trails between water courses, which are generally relatively short. However, weight is still an issue, so it is best to avoid any canned foods that can be more lightly transported in a dried form, such as soups and vegetables. Look instead for sustaining foods that will contribute more significantly to a meal, such as canned fish and meats or canned fruit, which are a real morale booster. It is also wonderful, of course, to supplement ingredients with fish caught on rod and line.

COOKING EQUIPMENT

The canoe camp is extremely mobile, so I carry very basic tools in a small tool roll. Essential daily ingredients live in small leather sacks (small dry bags will serve the same purpose) lined with ziplock bags. All of these ingredients are transported in a larger, strong dry bag.

Here again, only sufficient ingredients for the day are kept close by the fire; the bulk is stored securely in a food pack or blue barrel.

MULTI-DAY HIKING

Hiking requires us to carry our rations on our backs all day. Lightweight rations are the answer. Here, specially prepared rations are the way to go, whether they are shop-bought or homemade. Commercial trail rations have the advantage that they have been carefully designed for the needs of expeditions, are conveniently packaged and provide adequate nutrition. However, while they are now available in menus to suit diverse cultural dietary requirements, they remain limited in their scope for hikers with specific food allergies, in which case it is best if the hiker makes their own rations.

Commercial trail rations fall into two main types: ready-to-eat meals and freeze-dried meals, both of which are supported with dried foods such as biscuits and oatmeal blocks, along with beverages.

READY-TO-EAT RATIONS

Ready-to-eat rations are pre-cooked and have a long shelf life – usually around three years. Conveniently packaged in pouches, they can be eaten cold or heated by placing the pouch in hot water, or even in a flameless ration heater. I like these convenient rations for day hiking and when watching wildlife for prolonged periods. Their drawbacks are their weight and that, unless protected, they will freeze in sub-zero conditions.

FREEZE-DRIED RATIONS

Assuming that water is available, dehydrated rations, which are not prone to freezing and have the best calorie-to-weight ratio, are the best option for multi-day hiking, especially if you have the foraging skills to supplement the ration with wild herbs, shellfish or fungi. When cooking dehydrated rations, for good flavour, be sure to allow sufficient cooking time.

When I am using prepared ration packs, while packing I religiously strip out any unnecessary packaging and unwanted items. In nearly all cases, I carry my own brew kit rather than the usually disappointing and insufficient beverage component of a field ration. Brews are important for health and morale, so both quality and quantity are valued.

DIY RATIONS

It is also possible to create your own rations from selected items from the supermarket. Commercial trail rations have long shelf lives, but since you will be making your ration just prior to a trip, this is not essential. Look for foods that you like, that are available in small sizes and that are quick to cook. A shorter cooking time means less fuel to carry. Obviously, if you have allergies or dietary requirements, factor those in too.

It is surprising how much is available when a long shelf life is not essential. However, as you will discover, it is difficult to build a sustaining 24-hour ration that weighs less than 1kg. Fortunately, it is now possible to purchase specialist trail ration components separately, which you can combine in your own ration formulation.

CALCULATING RATIONS

When calculating quantities, bear in mind that for strenuous outdoor activity you will need more than the amount manufacturers specify as a normal serving. For example, on a canoe trip, I will begin the day with three sachets of quick-cook oats, two when hiking. A favourite meal is noodles with a tin of mackerel fillets. But here, make up the noodles using extra water to increase the volume of the broth; at the end of a day's hiking we are usually more dehydrated than we realise.

above The wilderness chef must be versatile and adaptable: one moment they may be cooking in a cabin, in another from the back of a Landrover, and at other times with no utensils at all.

WATER

Water is a fundamental of life and the number one resource of outdoor cooking – from cleaning hands, surfaces and food to its use as an ingredient. Any water used for cooking must be safe. Water collected from the wild or, for that matter, any suspect source, should be treated to remove any particulate matter, waterborne pathogens, bacteria and viruses. Wherever possible, search for a reliable source of water that's as clear as possible and preferably flowing.

Unfortunately, waterborne hazards are microscopic – invisible to the human eye. On expeditions, I therefore use a variety of filtration methods to remove the larger hazards, such as harmful protozoa and bacteria, and boil and chemically disinfect the water to destroy viruses.

PARTICULATE MATTER

This is visible matter in the water that can make it appear cloudy or milky. It can be caused by mineral or vegetable particles or by algae. This

below A native American cooking technique, improvising a wind shield to provide more control of the cooking fire.

material can shield harmful organisms from chemical disinfection, may interfere with the chemical used for the water disinfection or, in the case of glacial grit, may directly cause irritation to the intestine if ingested. Particulates also clog water filters, reducing their flow rate.

The best option is to search for a water source free from this sort of contamination. Failing that, the water should be filtered through cloth. Here, there are two very good methods:

1   Light contamination can be prefiltered through a sheet of parachute nylon. To do this, stretch a piece of nylon over a large billycan and secure it with a piece of nylon cord. Water from the wild is then ladled through this and the resulting (much clearer) water is then passed through a more comprehensive filter (see below).
2   Seriously muddy water will need more effective prefiltering, for which I use an army Millbank bag. This is a slow filtration method and will impinge on any fancy culinary ambitions.

PROTOZOA AND BACTERIA

At 1 micron in size, both protozoa and bacteria are large enough to be removed by filtration. Over the years, I have used an astonishing array of filters. It appears that about each decade a new water treatment technology becomes available. Currently, I am using hollow-fibre filters. These are highly effective, but only as long as they are operated according to the manufacturer's specifications, particularly in regard to back flushing. On day hikes, I use a small hand pump filter. In hike camps and canoe camps, I prefer a gravity feed filter.

VIRUSES

Much smaller than protozoa and bacteria, viruses range in size from 0.5–2 microns and are difficult to remove by filtration.

Fortunately, in most wilderness areas, viruses are a minor threat. It is when near to human communities, particularly where there are rudimentary sewage arrangements, that they become an issue.

Although viruses can be filtered out using top-of-the-line water purifiers, such as the excellent MSR Guardian, there is wisdom in post-filtration chemical treatment or boiling. All of these water filtration systems require correct handling, and with human error being such as it is, boiling and disinfecting filtered water provides a belt to support our braces and ensure viruses do not survive.

DISINFECTION

Chemical disinfection

Currently the most widely used chemical for disinfecting water is chlorine. When using chemical water treatments, ensure that you follow the instructions to ensure the correct dosage and the correct contact time. Water bottles and jerry cans should have the cap threads flushed with treated water after disinfecting.

Disinfection by boiling

To purify water by boiling, bring the water to a rolling boil and continue boiling for 1 minute. Longer boiling over a stove is just a waste of fuel.

HYGIENE

There is a misconception that outdoor cooking is grubby by nature, immune in some way from the risks and hazards of civilised cooking. This is not the case. In fact, quite the reverse is true: outdoors, we must pay even greater attention to hygiene and food handling. The very nature of living outdoors means that we are nearly always living in the perfect circumstances for food contamination and the growth of bacteria. To stay safe requires vigilance and the application of some common-sense principles.

CLEAN HANDS

Our hands are the source of the greatest risk of cross-contamination. It is vitally important that they are kept clean when handling food or cooking utensils. Proper washing with hot water and antibacterial soap is the preference. No fixed camp is properly equipped unless it has hand-washing facilities.

Any cuts must also be kept scrupulously clean and bandaged. Equip the fixed camp kitchen with highly visible finger dressings.

HANDLING WATER CONTAINERS

To avoid cross-contamination, I run a regime in my camp that stipulates that no one with dirty hands can open a jerry can and caps are always replaced immediately. Water containers must also periodically be disinfected.

SURFACES, UTENSILS AND CONTAINERS

All outdoor meals begin and end with hot water: hot water to use when washing the equipment, tools and surfaces prior to cooking; and hot water to wash up with at the end of the meal.

In a fixed camp, it is possible to have cutting boards for each food group, but in simpler back-country settings this is impractical. Instead, plan the meal so that any raw foods are handled separately, and the cutting tools, containers and any surfaces that have come into contact with the raw food are thoroughly cleansed before subsequent use.

SAFE FOOD STORAGE

Although refrigeration is viable during 4x4 expeditions, I still prefer not to store food after a meal. Instead, meals need to be carefully planned to avoid waste, served immediately when they are ready and still piping hot, and leftovers should be disposed of rather than stored since they are a potential source of bacterial infection.

Wherever possible, I prefer to obtain fresh food as necessary, even when camp refrigeration is available. The worst case of food poisoning I have suffered resulted from meat being stored for too long in a camp refrigerator on a desert expedition. The camp cook should have ditched the meat but thought he could press one more day from it. Cheers for that! It is not necessary: canned or dried goods can bridge the periods when fresh ingredients are not available.

THE 'ANDY HANDY'

Perhaps the most important piece of equipment in the camp kitchen, be it elaborate or simple, is a Andy Handy. This is a simple gravity tap operated with a spigot that can be attached to a bucket and suspended. Raising the spigot causes the water to flow, providing an excellent tap for cleaning dirty hands. I fit an Andy Handy to a small dry bag (5 litres), to which I attach a small bar of antibacterial soap contained in a small section of mosquito net.

With this set-up, I have water and soap always on hand, enabling hand cleaning after dressing meat or fish. Empty, this handy tap can be carried in a trouser pocket. Consequently, it lives permanently in the lid pocket of my pack. I even use it for a shower, filling the dry bag with suitably warmed water.

POTS, PANS AND KETTLES

We will cover the types and uses of pots and pans in more detail in the chapters on specific cooking techniques – such as in cast iron, frying and boiling – that follow, but here's a brief overview of the different types to serve as a guide when planning your kit for an expedition.

THE BILLYCAN

The billycan is the most versatile and therefore the most important cooking utensil. These come in many shapes and sizes. My preference is for stainless-steel billies, which must be fitted with a bail arm for suspension above a heat source.

Tall billycans will sit well pushed into the edge of a fire and are good for all cooking that is based upon boiling. They are the true back-country billies. A lid is an advantage, keeping ash and detritus out of the meal.

Broad pans are better suited to more ambitious forms of outdoor cooking. These are best suspended above the heat source and provide excellent access to the pan base, enabling easier monitoring of the cooking. They are great for sauces, soups and stews.

THE FRYING PAN

A frying pan is the second-most important pan in the outdoor kitchen. It provides a quick means to cook a wide range of foods, including bannock – a type of bread. In the home kitchen, it is usual to have a good thick-based pan that retains some heat and, most importantly, distributes that heat evenly. However, in the outdoors, excepting the fixed camp, we have to compromise for reasons of compactness and lightness. You can choose from a range of frying pans made from a variety of materials, each with different benefits.

Cast iron

This can be used to make a heavy, robust pan that heats slowly but retains heat well. It is ideal for searing meats and the cooking of robust foods. Heat distribution is optimal in cast iron, providing a lovely even cooking surface. Bare iron is corrodible when used with acidic foods and must be seasoned before use (see page 32). The weight, though, is the issue; even in a fixed camp, a cast-iron frying pan is excessive.

below Large heavy pots and specialised coffee pots are bulky and cumbersome but open a world of culinary possibilities for cooking in a fixed camp. If travelling by vehicle and there is the space, the answer is always...yes.

Besides, we have the lid from our camp or Dutch oven, which can be used in its stead.

Steel or black iron

Heavy steel or black-iron pans heat more quickly than cast-iron ones, but still allow for good heat distribution. Being much lighter, they are the best choice for the fixed camp or vehicle-transported field kitchen. They are corrodible so must also be seasoned (see page 32), but this is no drawback. Their robustness is perfect for outdoor cooking. In the fixed camp, it is wise to have two pans: a large one suitable for cooking for your group, and a more modest-sized one for other times. Look for a pan with an angled wall and that is

not too shallow, so that sauces and gravies can be made in it.

Lightweight steel pans can also be found, sometimes with folding handles, sometimes with sockets for the fitting of a wooden handle. My personal favourite pan is a moderately thin iron one with a folding handle. It has a good shaped edge and sufficient depth to hold a bannock when tilted towards the fire. It has been a constant companion on many arduous canoe expeditions and seems to get better with age.

above A lightweight cooking set for vehicle travel, comprising a nesting set of stainless-steel billy cans, large, medium and small, a kettle, two lightweight frying pans and some plates. The whole set occupies next to no space and keeps culinary options open.

Aluminium

The advantage of aluminium is that it's lightweight. Outdoor aluminium frying pans come in several varieties: the thick anodised or non-stick pans and the ultra-thin pans such as that supplied in the Trangia system. The thick pans often have a folding handle and are pretty good for cooking over a stove or making a bannock beside the fire. That said, I am sceptical about the use of non-stick coatings outdoors. These do not cope well with the high temperatures prevalent in cooking on a campfire. I am not saying they cannot be used, just that it requires skill, and then consider that the least experienced outdoor cook is the person most likely to reach for the non-stick frying pan...

USING AN ULTRA-THIN PAN

Despite its thinness, the Trangia pan can be used well. In recent years, non-stick and hard-anodised pans have become available, although my favourite are the stainless-steel-lined Trangia Duossal pans. Whichever you opt for, using an ultra-thin pan requires less heat and more skill, along with constant concentration; the pan must be kept moving to ensure an even spread of heat from the small burner.

below My very well-travelled canoe camp cook set. Canoe travel can be especially hard on equipment so make sure you purchase good quality pans with solid rivets. Ideal for cooking for two or three people, my set comprises a medium and small stainless billy can, a 1-litre stainless-steel kettle and a small bannock pan with a folding handle. Utensils, spoons or spatulas can be carved from driftwood.

Stainless steel

In the home, stainless-steel pans come with heavy bases to provide even heat distribution. However, stainless-steel pans designed for outdoor use are very thin and must also be kept moving in use to prevent scorching and the food sticking. Their only advantage is their resistance to corrosion.

SEASONING IRON PANS

Iron and carbon-steel pans are porous. For this reason, they must be seasoned to seal the pores, help to prevent rust forming and create a more non-stick surface. Seasoning pans is easy and is covered in later chapters, but since it is vital to the maintenance of your kit from time to time between expeditions, here's a brief overview of how to do it for different types of pots and pans:

1 To begin with, wash the pot or pan three times with very hot water. This is especially important for new utensils, which will be protected with a thick layer of wax. By all means use a small quantity of washing detergent.
2 Rinse the pot or pan very well, then dry it thoroughly.

For a wok or frying pan:

1 Heat the pan until a splash of water immediately vaporises. Add sufficient oil – choose one with a high smoke point (see page 104) – to cover the whole surface.
2 Reduce the heat, add some sliced onions and fry, ensuring that all of the pan surface is covered, until soft. Do not allow the onion to burn.
3 Discard the onion and allow the pan to cool.
4 Rinse out with hot water, dry and repeat the process twice more.
5 Finally give the pan a wipe over with a very lightly oiled piece of kitchen paper.

For cast-iron pot or pan:

1 On a dry day, set a griddle over a good fire of charcoal. Heat the washed pan until very hot then, using oven gloves and a set of tongs, wipe all of the pan's surfaces, inside and out, with a piece of kitchen paper soaked in oil (with a high smoke point) or vegetable shortening.
2 Place the oven upside down on the griddle and cook until it stops smoking.
3 Remove from the heat and allow to cool.

MAINTAINING POTS AND PANS

To maintain your pots and pans, periodically repeat the seasoning process. Do not be perturbed by the doom monger or naysayer, quick to pronounce a pan ruined if it is washed with detergent; iron and carbon steel are in truth very forgiving materials and easy to live with. All of us who have used them hard on remote expeditions laugh at such folly, while reaching for a pinch of salt.

THE KETTLE

A kettle is a wonderfully evocative cooking utensil; somehow, the suspended kettle sings of well-being. I prefer Scandinavian-style kettles, which are designed for the outdoors and have a short, almost non-existent spout and a low, flat profile. This shape is easily transported in a pack. Ensure the kettle is fitted with a cover to prevent soot covering everything the kettle comes into contact with when travelling.

If you are going to boil a lot of coffee, a dedicated coffee pan is the way to go. The old-timers would insist that it never be more than rinsed out, the flavour of the coffee improving with age. I shall leave you to make your own determination on that.

A FLAME TO COOK OVER

I have lost count of the many different stoves I have used outdoors. As time has gone on, new materials and ideas have constantly superseded older models. Some stoves I lived with for a few years have been forgotten, while the earliest stoves I used, fondly remembered marvels in brass, are now found mostly in museums, the technology of a bygone era. Interestingly, as my experience has grown, so too has my attitude to stoves. Here are the stoves I use the most; nothing too fancy, just models that are rugged, reliable and that have stood the test of time.

THE CAMPFIRE

The original stove, the campfire, remains the most versatile heat source for cooking. However, managing a fire is a skilful business that takes many years to learn and master. Yet I still love cooking over a fire, above all stoves.

Sadly, though, there are increasing regulations and prohibitions on the use of fires. Whether prohibition of the carbon neutral campfire is justifiable is worthy of a long debate for another occasion.

THE TRANGIA STOVE

While bulky, the Trangia stove set-up is one of my favourites; I carry one in my off-road vehicle as a matter of course. Quick and easy to get going, it is ideal for using for a refreshing brew but also supports real culinary aspirations, enabling the cooking of proper sauce-based dishes.

The design is incredibly stable and provides wonderful protection from the wind. The stove can also be used with a variety of burners. The original spirit burner is simple, elegant and works. I like it for its lack of moving parts, the cleanliness of the ethanol fuel and particularly

above The Trangia cookset is a favourite. Although a little bulky, it provides a lightweight, stable and versatile cooking platform.

its silence. Yes, it is a little slow when raced against other stoves, but how often are we racing? When I need a more energy-efficient fuel, I exchange the spirit burner for the multi-fuel burner, which allows me to use a wide range of fuels with quicker cooking times. My preferred fuel is Coleman fuel.

THE COLEMAN DOUBLE BURNER

These stoves have been the stalwart in the tents of Inuit hunters and Northern First Nations seemingly forever. Simple, tough and reliable, they just do the job. With spare parts readily available for servicing, in theory, they can live forever.

OUTFITS

DAY-HIKE OUTFIT

- military metal mug with water bottle
- mug lid
- stove support stand
- spirit burner
- brew kit
- fuel bottle
- ration pack
- spoon
- Swiss Army knife
- Woodlore Fire Stick

This is my cooking outfit for day hiking and is without a doubt the outfit that sees the most use. It is sufficiently compact, quick and easy to use and it allows me to stop and conjure a fresh hot beverage at will. Unsurprisingly, it lives permanently in my small day pack.

Rather than relying on a thermal flask, which can only contain a limited supply of warm water or beverage, I prefer to carry a very lightweight stove. A small quantity of fuel will allow me to boil many litres of water. Should you become stranded overnight in bad weather, through injury or navigational error, access to sweet, hot drinks can save a life. Actually, I have many times used this outfit for much longer, relying also on the Scout Cooking techniques covered later (see pages 51–87).

As you can see, for this outfit I rely on a trusty Trangia burner. The brew kit is a small dry bag filled with sachet beverages and coffee bags.

MULTI-DAY HIKE OUTFIT

Solo

- day-hike outfit (see opposite)
- Littlbug Junior Stove
- 12cm (about 5in) billycan
- titanium pan
- larger fuel supply
- rations

Multi-day hiking *can* be achieved with the day-hike outfit but it is very limiting. Simply carrying a second cooking vessel is a welcome benefit at mealtimes. My set, as with all things, is constructed with items from different manufacturers. The billycan is stainless steel and only 12cm (about 5in) in diameter. I could use a lighter pot, but quite frankly, I prefer the robustness of the stainless steel both in terms of swinging it above a fire and its ability to cope with the rough treatment it will receive on a rough expedition.

Inside it I carry a Littlbug Junior Stove. This lightweight marvel disassembles to fit snugly inside the billycan, so it occupies virtually no space. Once assembled, it provides a wide, stable base for the billycan to sit on and can be set to cook with a Trangia burner or by burning small sticks, which it does incredibly well. This stove occupies so little space that I can also fit inside it – like a Russian doll – a titanium pot containing a bail arm and mug handle, as well as a brew kit and Trangia stove.

Wherever possible, carry billycans with bail arms so that they can be suspended over a fire.

Two people

- mug and water bottles for each person
- Trangia 25 cookset
- spirit burner or multi-fuel burner, depending on temperature and trip duration
- rations or basic foodstuffs

When you travel as a party of two you must decide whether or not you each carry an individual cooking outfit or whether to share a single outfit. If you are going to stick together throughout your journey, the latter is lighter, which means there is good news: you can carry more or fresher food supplies.

With campfires prohibited in the majority of national parks, the stove I use is a Trangia 25 cookset. I will admit that for many years I disliked it, but now that the Duossal stainless-steel lined pans are available, over time they have become a real favourite.

CANOE CAMP OUTFIT

- mug and water bottles for each person
- stainless-steel kettle
- black iron frying pan
- stainless-steel billycan set
- tool roll
- small cutting board
- rations

On most canoe trips it is possible to cook on an open fire. (When fire restrictions are in place, I use the Trangia 25 cookset already described.) Open-fire cooking is hard on cooking pots, so invest in a good set of stainless-steel billycans with strong bail arms fitted, and with steel rivets rather than aluminium ones, which have a tendency to melt. The set I use has been cobbled

VEHICLE FLY CAMP OUTFIT

- mug and water bottles for each person
- large billycan set
- large kettle
- Bedourie oven
- frying pan
- coffee percolator
- Atago stove
- tripod

The vehicle fly camp is a quick, lightweight camp, but with a vehicle to transport our equipment we can indulge ourselves. The Atago stove is ideal for this set-up as it is environmentally friendly and leaves no trace.

together over the years and has seen very heavy use. The canoe camp outfit is perfect for two to three people, but would need another billycan to cater to four. It assumes that each person, as always, has their own mug and water bottles.

The small kitchen tool roll is light and convenient. My basic food ingredients travel in ziplock bag-lined leather pouches in a dry bag. These are replenished as necessary from a large food pack or barrel. This system has evolved over many trips and is designed to be as simple as possible. Despite this, there is little culinary limitation with this outfit, any limitation arising from a lack of ingredients.

FIXED CAMP OUTFIT

- mug and water bottles for each person
- large billycan set
- full kitchen
- *potjie*
- camp oven
- folding griddle
- tripod

The fixed camp list looks small, but in terms of cooking utensils, these are all the heavy hitters. The sky is the limit in terms of cooking with this outfit.

FUNDAMENTAL COOKING SKILLS AND INGREDIENTS

Aside from roasting, frying, griddling and the like, there are some techniques and types of dish that span several categories of cooking, proving their versatility and elevating simple dishes from the mundane to the memorable. These include sauces, soups and curries – the mainstays of pan cooking – along with bakes and breads to accompany or follow them. All of these types of food are simple enough to make once you know how, but require some knowledge and certain ingredients for them to be truly successful.

SAUCES

At its most basic, a sauce creates cohesion for a dish; at best, a sauce is transformational, elevating the dish to a whole new level of gastronomic delight. Sauces, quite literally, are the heart and soul of good cooking.

Every cook – be they cooking in the galley of a small boat or in the draughty vestibule of a mountain tent – will benefit from a good repertoire of sauces. Being able to make them also teaches a deeper understanding of cooking, the manipulation of ingredients and flavours, which is perhaps most vital at those times when we have only limited ingredients and must improvise.

Of course, out of practical necessity there will be many occasions when we will be forced to live on pre-packaged trail rations. But at other times, our aspiration should be to always cook amazing meals outdoors. In the Appendix, I have set down a range of sauces I have found to be useful on expedition. Some can readily be made on a hike stove while others are better suited to a fixed camp. I make no apology for this, for in the course of one expedition you may find yourself cooking in a lodge one day, a cabin another and under the stars another. While the equipment and ingredients we can have with us at these times will vary, what does not are the culinary principles we employ.

If the culinary experts will forgive my simplification, sauces comprise three parts: the stock, the aromatics and the thickening component.

Stock

For the most part, we can rely solely upon dehydrated stock cubes or powders. However, because stock is so fundamental, I have included recipes, too, since it is easy to make them. What's more, the joy of making your own stock is not just that you capture wonderful flavours, but also that you make full and respectful use of your ingredients. Also, as always with cooking from scratch, you'll know what is in the food you are eating and can control the seasoning (especially the salt levels).

Aromatics

The basic vegetables, herbs and spices we use in sauces (and other dishes) are vital ingredients. Many of these can now be transported in a dehydrated form, but it pays to be aware that some of the peelings and parts of vegetables discarded in the preparation of other dishes can be used as flavouring agents for sauces and stocks.

Thickening

The methods of thickening covered in the soup section on page 44 can all be used in the thickening of sauces, along with two other methods: thickening with blood, or a paste made of equal parts flour and butter called a beurre manié.

Blood thickening is a less popular method in today's world, but in remote wilderness it still plays an important role. One of the most impressive things I have seen was watching an old Cree man cook a rabbit stew with little more than a spoonful of lard, a spoonful of flour, salt and cold water. For flavour, colour and thickening he squeezed every last drop of blood from the liver into the billycan. While his dish would have benefited from thyme and some sweated onion, carrot and celery (mirepoix), under the circumstances in which it was eaten – a remote hunter's cabin filled with 50 years' worth of bric-a-brac, with the thermometer hitting -37°C outside and a smoky, rust-perforated wood-burning stove lifting the mercury to life-supporting comfort inside – I can tell you, it was fine dining.

A beurre manié is a rich way to both thicken and gloss a sauce at the end of the cooking process, and is widely used in classic French cooking. The method itself is sound, but what I think is more important is the concept of finishing a sauce – seasoning with salt and pepper, balancing any bitterness with a dash of honey or sugar – while also improving its visual appeal and consistency.

CREATING FLAVOUR

Perhaps the most important concept to take away from this section is the importance of capturing every atom of flavour from the ingredients – particularly in searching out those wonderful brown meat residues that coat the base of pans and roasting trays and liberating them with a glass of water or wine to capture their essence.

Those intense flavours result from a process called the Maillard reaction. This is the interaction between amino acids and sugars that generates new flavour molecules and aromas – a heady mixture that transports us back to the day when a long-distant ancestor first cooked some meat over a flame. Can you imagine the flavour explosion in the mouth of someone who had only ever until that moment eaten their food raw? It's that unique flavour that you should try to capture in your sauces. If you manage that, you can't go far wrong.

SOUPS

'ce, qui répare les forces, aliment ou remède fortifiant'

('this, which restores strength, a fortifying food or remedy')

GUILLAUME BRIÇONNET ET MARGUERITE D'ANGOULÊME, CORRESPONDANCE (1521–1524)

Soup... Such a simple word, such a simple food. Soup has been made for as long as we have had the ability to boil ingredients. However, while it was certainly possible to make soup using skin or basketry vessels and heated rocks, it would have been the invention of the cooking pot that truly revolutionised the process. And the cooking pot goes back a long way in human history: scorched

pot fragments found at the Xianren Cave, China, bear witness to the use of pots for cooking in 20,000 BC – 10,000 years before the adoption of agriculture. Soup is ancient food indeed.

We can only guess at those early recipes, but if we could travel back in time, I am sure we would find the same sense of comfort rising in the aroma from those ancient pots as we find rising from ours today. For despite its simplicity, soup has long been a nourishing and life-saving food that makes efficient use of ingredients both in terms of their nutrition and flavour. During the Siege of Leningrad during the Second World War, for instance, soup was a culinary lifeline in the beleaguered city. Lasting 900 days, it is believed that some 800,000 people starved to death during the siege. With little food available, necessity became the mother of invention, and out of sheer desperation, soup was made from all manner of unlikely ingredients, even wallpaper stripped from the walls; the paper had been hung with potato starch glue, which, when softened by boiling, could be scraped from the paper and used as a soup base.

Aside, perhaps, from ones made from wallpaper paste, the wholesome quality of soup has long been recognised. In 16th-century France, for example, a broth that was sold on the streets was called 'restaurant', in acknowledgement of its restorative quality. By the 18th century, establishments were opened that specialised in serving these restoring broths, and thus the modern 'restaurant' was born.

We shall follow this gastronomic genesis as wilderness chefs, for beyond the obvious nutritional benefits, preparing fresh soup introduces important culinary techniques and encourages experimentation: soups can be adapted to a wide range of ingredients, including those foraged in the wild. But most importantly of all, soup making encourages us to pay respect to our ingredients and develops the delicacy of culinary touch necessary to maximise their flavours.

Fresh vs. dried soups

Expediently compact and lightweight, it is completely understandable that outdoor travellers usually fall back on powdered, dehydrated packet soups for convenience. If I am travelling very light, I will often carry some sachets of concentrated miso soup, but always I look to the wild to furnish additional foraged ingredients to reinforce the base stock, even if it is only a few humble nettle tops.

However, compared to a freshly made soup, the powdered variety is little more than flavoured water. What's more, making a fresh soup is fun, rewarding and a culinary delight. It is not always the case that we are travelling so lightly that we cannot make a soup from fresh ingredients. We may be working out of a cabin, hostel, outdoor education centre or even aboard a small boat. Under these circumstances, we have the great opportunity to make fresh and hearty soup to suit our needs, preferences and the ingredients available.

Maximising flavour

Soup making is all about flavour and to this end I encourage you to stay alert to the availability of the freshest ingredients with significant flavour potential. The recipes included in the Boiling chapter (see pages 141–97) represent the way I cook in perfect circumstances; my methods pay homage to the great chefs of the past who mastered the techniques of capturing flavour, while at the same time taking inspiration from

HOW TO FINELY CHOP AN ONION

1 Slice the onion in half between its ends.

2 Make many slices vertically through each half.

3 Cut once or twice horizontally two thirds of the way through each half.

4 Slice downwards across the prepared cuts to produce the diced onion.

'nouveau cuisine', the new culinary masters who cook quickly to preserve nutrients and colour. Quick cooking, of course, also favours the wilderness chef, who may be using a hiking stove with a limited fuel supply.

Personally, I find that cooking a soup outside is a total joy, almost an act of religious devotion, especially when I am cooking for a group of my fellow outdoor enthusiasts. The responsibility is to honour my guests, by honouring the potential of the wonderful ingredients available; as the chef, I am merely a conduit connecting people with nature.

While it is true that sometimes on expeditions I may have to make do with preserved ingredients rather than fresh, or make substitutions for missing ingredients, the inspiration and methodology I employ is classical and even with poor ingredients, good cooking produces good results.

Ingredient preparation

Soup making requires a considerable amount of ingredient preparation, mostly in the chopping up of vegetables. It is worth taking the time to learn the techniques for dicing ingredients. Perhaps most important of all is the ability to produce a quick and very fine dice, the fine 'brunoise' of the French kitchen. Modern soup recipes frequently call for a blender to puree the soup towards the end of the cooking, but a blender is not available to us outdoors, so we must compensate by preparing our ingredients very finely prior to cooking them. Some of these will dissolve in the cooking, others will not, but all will lend a charming, rustic appeal to the soup. Also, finely chopped ingredients cook more swiftly and create a lesser demand for fuel. You will find the necessary knife skills for this technique shown above.

In my cooking *sous le ciel*, 'under the sky', I have one overall guiding principle, which is to always defy the preconception that outdoor cooking is inferior to indoor cooking.

The flavour base

As you will discover, nearly all soups, sauces, stews and casseroles are constructed on a basic base of flavour. Classically, this is a mixture of diced onion, celery and carrot that is sweated in butter or oil over gentle heat until soft and translucent, but not coloured. In French cooking, this is called a 'mirepoix'. The components of the mirepoix can vary according to the recipe and what is available. For example, I sometimes substitute peeled marsh thistle stem for the celery. When cooking delicately flavoured soups, consider using milder base ingredients such as shallots, rather than onions. A really good start to your soup comes from this early phase, when a strongly flavoured paste is achieved before you add the bulk of the stock. It is vitally important not to burn the ingredients; this is more of a concern when we are cooking outdoors with very thin-based pots and pans. If you are worried that conditions do not allow sufficient control, add a couple of spoonfuls of the stock at this early stage to reduce the risk of scorching the mirepoix. A burned soup base is a disaster and will produce a soup with a burnt flavour.

Herbs

I always prefer to use the freshest ingredients, so much so that I have developed a passion for camping in those landscapes in which herbs grow wild in nature. These include the mountains of Provence, where both wild thyme and wild rosemary can easily be found. That being said, on expedition, dried herbs weigh nothing and can easily be transported, and will elevate any dish to new heights.

Herbs that are adapted to hot climates, such as thyme, bay, rosemary, sage and oregano, are less likely to wilt in the outdoor kitchen.

To extract the greatest benefit from them, introduce them to your dish early on, when sweating down your soup base in fat or oil. This will liberate the aromatic essential oils from the leaf glands. The more delicate herbs, such as fresh coriander, parsley, basil and tarragon, are more prone to wilting and therefore less useful in a mobile outdoor kitchen. If you do use them, they are best added late in the cooking process. Wild mint can frequently be found in the wild, along with many other edible wild herbs, which, although less flavoursome than the classic kitchen herbs, can be used as a fresh garnish.

Dried herbs should be stored in air- and light-tight containers. When using them, go easy on the quantity and taste the dish carefully. Too much of a dried herb can spoil the soup.

BOUQUET GARNI

Personally, I am not a fussy diner and am quite happy to fish out a bay leaf or thyme stem from my food, particularly if it is delicious. But not everyone feels the same way. Consequently, it is worth learning to make a bouquet garni. This is a small bundle of herbs – bay leaf, thyme sprig and chervil – sandwiched between two pieces of celery and tied with string. It can easily be recovered from the soup before serving. However, I have never taken chervil into an outdoor kitchen, so instead I substitute the leaves of the celery and for string, I normally use the fibres from a nettle stem.

Spices

Spices are usually purchased pre-dried. For this reason, they are superbly suited to outdoor travel. As with dried herbs, they are best stored in air- and light-tight containers. Spices release their aromas most effectively in hot oil and are consequently usually added early in the cooking process. Some spices, such as star anise and cloves, can be used whole, while cardamom can be sufficiently crushed between two smooth rocks or with the back of an axe; otherwise, pre-ground spices are the most convenient for use. However, take care when using them as they are prone to burn easily, especially when we are using thin, highly conductive cooking vessels.

Thickening methods

REDUCTION

The simplest way to thicken a soup, sauce or curry is to reduce it. This means to continue cooking it so that the liquid evaporates. This will intensify the flavour of the dish, and it is for this reason that it is often normal to add salt late in the cooking process. The downsides are that reduction is costly in terms of fuel on a hike stove and it reduces the volume of food available.

FLOUR

The classic way to thicken soups and sauces is to use a cooked flour-and-fat paste called a roux. To make a roux, equal quantities of plain flour and melted butter or oil are mixed in a pan and then cooked for a couple of minutes to cook out the raw flour taste, at which point it also develops a lovely nutty aroma. As the roux darkens, it becomes less effective as a thickener, but provides a dark base for the soup or sauce.

Roux are cooked to three degrees:

1 a white roux, which is just cooked enough to remove the flour taste but remains pale
2 a blonde roux, which as its name suggests, is a golden colour
3 a brown roux, which has the most intense flavour of all

Roux is usually made in a separate pan and allowed to cool before being dissolved into piping hot stock. This avoids lumps forming. If time is short, I will instead add a small quantity of hot stock to the warm roux and whisk this in until it's smooth before adding this thinned roux to the main stock. Alternatively, if you have only one pot available, the flour can be added to the cooked mirepoix and stirred in to make a lumpy paste.

You will find all of these methods in the soup, sauce and curry recipes, but if you can, I recommend making a roux independently of the mirepoix at least once so that you understand how the flavour changes when the flour is correctly cooked through.

CORNFLOUR OR ARROWROOT POWDER

Cornflour or arrowroot powder can be used to thicken a soup, sauce or curry. To do so, dilute 2 tsp cornflour or arrowroot powder in 2 tsp cold water, mixing carefully to remove lumps. Whisk this into the hot mixture and cook for a few minutes. Arrowroot has twice the thickening effect of cornflour and many health benefits.

POTATOES

Potatoes are a wonderful way to thicken any soup as they readily dissolve in cooking; cut small, they easily disintegrate when whisked. This is also an area where dehydrated potato flakes or powder can be used. Go easy on the quantity though or your soup will turn into a solid flavoured mash.

RICE

Rice can be used as a soup thickener without interfering with the soup flavour. To do this, boil some rice until it is very overcooked, then use the cooking liquid to thicken your soup, having first strained out the rice grains.

DAIRY PRODUCTS

Soup can be thickened and enriched with a variety of dairy products. Cream, crème fraîche, sour cream, milk, evaporated milk and powdered milk can all be used.

Alternative ingredients

For the soup recipes, I am assuming that you have access to fresh ingredients. However, it may well be the case that these are simply not available. This need not interfere with your cooking, for today more than ever before we have access to all manner of dried or preserved ingredients that are suitable for lightweight or expedition travel – dehydrated vegetables being a case in point; I have long utilised these on jungle expeditions. The best results are obtained by allowing the veg plenty of time to soak in water to rehydrate. I prefer to do this overnight, placing the vegetables in a small Nalgene bottle filled with water.

If you can recognise edible fungi and plants, it is wonderful to be able to use wild ingredients in soups and other dishes. I also often carry wild fungi that I have dried at home. However, it is of course important to gain proper training in wild-food identification; I have heard tragic tales of enthusiastic amateurs poisoning themselves in error. Equally, anglers, hunters and beachcombers can furnish their own fresh ingredients for a soup. That is the joy of soup making: it is so much about adapting a recipe to what is locally or seasonally available.

CURRIES

One of the most adaptable ways to conjure a tasty outdoor meal, cooking curries requires a different set of basic ingredients from those used for soups and sauces. The scope is almost limitless, in part because curry recipes vary widely by region, reflecting both the availability of ingredients, long cultural traditions and trading interactions. For example, in northern Thailand, the jungle curry exemplifies the environment in both its name and its design; these humble forest meals are created without coconut milk, which historically could only be obtained close to the far-distant coast.

Many curry sauces are general-purpose: they can be cooked as vegan or vegetarian dishes one day, as fish dishes the next and yet again with meat on another occasion. In the remote jungle, it is not uncommon to encounter curries containing wild frogs, snails or any other source of foraged edible protein. They also frequently contain edible roots, leaves and fungi garnered from the forest. The value of such culinary versatility should not be underestimated by a wilderness chef,

While no one would disagree that the best results come from using freshly ground spices, the truth is that dried spices are really not such a compromise, for they are extremely lightweight, taste wonderful and will stay fresh for months. What's more, it is very easy to create a portable spice supply in a small dry

ESSENTIAL SPICES

When I travel in the rainforest, I usually go equipped with this sort of spice kit, supplemented with dried fried onion, dried fried shrimp and other delicacies found in the local markets.

chaat masala	fish sauce
garam masala	cloves
ground turmeric	ground cinnamon
Malaysian curry powder for meat	ground coriander
chilli powder	ground cumin
ground ginger	kaffir lime leaves (dried)
cardamom pods	lemongrass (dried)

bag. The spices listed above will serve for all of the curries in this book, and more. They can be contained in small ziplock bags in a dry sack or in medicine bottles.

Keeping it simple

Curry recipes can be incredibly varied and are often exciting culinary extravaganzas, but for the purposes of this book, my interest is in the more modest dishes that can be cooked in one pot, with only the need for a handful of ingredients and, for the most part, the simple, portable spices listed above.

CAKES AND BAKING

Good news: there is always a need for sweet baking in the outdoors camp. After all, that is what birthdays are for. I can remember several times trying to conjure a cake of sorts in remote places with next to no ingredients, perhaps the hardest occasion being in a jungle village in the remote rainforest of Venezuela. All the food we had with us had been flown in at great expense and with a strict weight limit, so there were no luxury items to eat. Added to this was the difficulty of attempting to bake in the scorching heat and tropical humidity. I do not recall how the cake was made, but it was, and I adhered to the wilderness chef's mantra: 'Where there is a will, there will be a way.'

That said, although it is possible to bake in the jungle, there is no denying that outdoor baking reaches its zenith in the fixed expedition camp or ship's galley. I have kept the recipes very simple, for baking – wherever you do it – can be a demanding skill on expeditions. Increasingly,

AERATING FLOUR

When transporting flour into remote regions, it is inevitably heavily compressed within the sacks that contain it. To improve baking results, you therefore need to aerate the flour. In the home kitchen, this is achieved by sifting, but in the field we can use a whisk or a fork to agitate air back into the powder. This is more important than ever in the expedition kitchen, where we have little control over the ambient temperature.

BLIND BAKING

Enter the realm of baking and it is not long before the techniques increase in their complexity. Who can deny that a pie is wonderful when it has a pastry base to accompany the lid or that a quiche isn't better when its base is not soggy? To achieve these results, the pastry needs to be blind baked, which simply involves lining the baking dish with the pastry and baking it prior to filling.

1 With the pastry rolled out, begin by pre-warming the baking dish. This can be done over the fire.
2 Oil the dish so the pastry will release easily and then line it with the rolled-out pastry.
3 Brush the pastry with beaten egg or a mixture of 2 tsp powdered egg and 4 tsp water; this will help to seal the base and prevent it from going soggy.
4 Prick the base with a pointed stick or fork so that steam does not cause it to rise.
5 In addition, it is best to weight down the base while it bakes. You can do this by filling the base with uncooked rice, and I have even used smooth pea-sized pebbles that had been washed and sterilised prior to use. These can then be saved and used repeatedly, as can the rice.
6 Bake the pastry base in a hot camp oven for about 15 minutes, until light golden.
7 Fill the case as required, and bake as instructed.

though, 4x4 vehicles are being set up with fridges and freezers, making it ever easier to work with heat-shy pastry. Who knows what culinary marvels will grace the tables of the next generation of wilderness chefs?

Baking in a camp oven

When baking cakes, pies or quiches in a camp oven, a trivet arrangement is advisable. That is not to say you cannot manage without one, just that it will be far easier to get good results if you use one. I also prefer to bake in a large camp oven so that the cake is not so close to the walls. As always, go really easy with the heat; for the most part, baking requires an oven temperature of 180–200°C, although when baking bread it will be higher. One advantage of the Petromax camp oven is that the lid has a convenient port to allow the internal temperature to be measured with the aid of an instant-read thermometer. To do this, it is best to lift the oven off and away from the heat source. The iron will easily retain sufficient heat to carry on baking while you gauge the temperature.

BREAD

From the alluring aroma of its baking to the crisp crackle of a well-formed crust yielding reluctantly to the knife, bread has a beguiling hold on humanity. The very act of breaking bread with a stranger, a ritual of ancient negotiation, is still accepted as a sacred act of diplomacy that is respected in the modern age. This is because bread is deeply rooted in our psyche: it epitomises sharing, group effort, connection and well-being.

We have been making bread since our hunter-gatherer past, the earliest evidence so far recognised by archaeologists being charred remains in ovens found at the Shubayqa 1 site in the Black Desert of north-east Jordan. These remains suggest that unleavened breads were being baked from flour made from wild cereals and tubers well over 14,000 years ago. This should not come as a surprise though, for wild breads are still made by current hunter-gatherer societies. I like to think that it was while sharing a loaf of unleavened wild grain that the idea of agriculture was first suggested.

Bread for every occasion

Certainly, when we are outdoors, bread has a huge impact on morale. A wilderness chef should therefore be able to bake a variety of breads to suit different circumstances. When travelling with a lightweight fly camp, our bread-making aspirations are usually limited to bread leavened with baking powder – the soda breads. These are simple, quick to cook and require no specialised utensils. Virtually unaffected by the weather, they remain a practical solution for baking on the remote trail and are a wonderful introduction to bread making in a wider sense.

In the fixed or vehicle-transported camp, it is possible to construct an oven from rocks and mud or even to carry a field oven. However, in reality these options are slow and cumbersome. The better solution is simply to bring along an iron camp oven. At this point, our aspirations soar and we reach for yeast to fashion bread every crumb the equal of the artisanal bakers'.

Baking bread outdoors is neither difficult, nor a dark art. It does, however, require patience and practice. In an ideal world, we would carry a set of scales with us to measure our ingredients by weight. This is certainly the most reliable method since powdered ingredients, flour in particular, can become compressed in transit, making certain measurement by volume problematic. However, I have never yet carried scales on an expedition, nor have I ever seen them used in any other wilderness camp. In truth, with experience and some practice we manage fine with volume measurements, which is what I shall use here, although I also provide the weight in grams in case you do happen to have scales to hand.

The vagaries of travel

Flour can be easily transported in dry bags lined with polythene food bags. However, not all flour is the same: the quantity of protein in flour varies from country to country. It is important to be aware of this, as it can take you by surprise. In particular, the volume of water the flour absorbs can vary, so be aware that you may need to modify the recipes in response to the flour available to you. I have found carrying out a few experiments prior to departure to be the best solution. Once I get a feel for the flour's properties, it is baking as usual.

Making bread with yeast involves working with a living ingredient. This is wonderful, so do not be surprised if you find that you develop a passion for bread baking. For the recipes here, I have confined myself to the use of fast-action dried yeast, which is incredibly reliable and convenient. In the old days, though, it was not unusual for pioneers to carry a live yeast culture, using it to make sourdough bread. Simply for the economy of space, I shall not include this here, but I am sure that if you take to bread making you will soon be exploring sourdough recipes as well.

Outdoor baking is somewhat more complicated than baking indoors. For example, in a flash camp you might have a table on which to knead bread, but more often than not, this will not be the case. Happily, you can usually improvise a work surface by cleaning a canoe paddle, the hull of a canoe or even a 4x4 bonnet. With this potential lack of work surface in mind, however, I've included recipes that require no kneading and can actually be produced in a mixing bowl or at most on a cutting board.

Outdoors, we also have to contend with the effect of a cooling breeze. This can reduce the rising of the dough and cause uneven cooking of a loaf. It is always wise to prove dough in a

place that's protected from the wind, such as the vestibule of a tent. I religiously wrap a spare jersey around the mixing bowl when the yeast is working. Of course, on fine days or in warmer climes the weather can speed up the proving process, so take care not to overprove it in these circumstances. To ensure even baking, always rotate the camp oven through 90 degrees at least twice during the baking time.

Above all else have fun baking, and eating, bread. There will be the odd failure, but the successes will clearly outmatch those and with time, it will become second nature.

SCOUT COOKING

'**IN THESE LAKE-SIDE CAMPS** every one cooks for himself. The lumps of meat (when they are available) are impaled on a piece of stick sharpened at both ends, so that the lower point may be pushed into the ground at an angle, and keep the meat in position while it is toasted.' *ACROSS ARCTIC LAPLAND, CUTCLIFFE HYNE, 1898*

Over the hills and far away, there are times when we will travel light, outfitted with only a small billy or kettle, a bag of salt, perhaps a bag of coffee, a cup, a knife and maybe some flour. But far from being a disadvantage, this light outfit can be a liberating experience for the wilderness chef. Instead of the normal paraphernalia of the field kitchen, we can enjoy the utensils of our ancient ancestors: sticks, stones, mud and fire.

While these methods may seem primitive and spartan, they are actually some of the most exciting and rewarding cooking techniques I know. The fact that they survive in a world of induction hobs, microwaves and multi-fuel hike stoves bears witness to their enduring popularity. When I think back over the past 35 years of travelling in remote wilderness, I realise that they have rewarded me in extraordinary locations and in the company of some of the most interesting and positive-minded human beings.

For its success this style of cooking depends on maximising the inherent natural flavours of the ingredients. We bring our ingredients into the closest proximity to the fire when cooking in this way, so much so that the fire itself can be considered an ingredient. In no other field of bush cookery is intuitive judgement more essential to regulate the cooking times; practice and experience are essential to master these methods, so do not assume, as many do, that scout cooking is simple. Like all cooking, there is a right way, the path that leads to successful, delicious fare, while the other slapdash route leads to teeth blackened on charred cinders or even broken and upset stomachs too.

The purpose of this approach is to cook the food well with minimal fuss and without unnecessary complication. For that reason, I have avoided artificial scout cooking techniques found in woodcraft camps and have focused instead on techniques

time-honoured by First Nations, hunters, explorers, trackers and adventurers.

At no time will you find me recommending the use of aluminium foil; while this can simplify many techniques, it is my fervent belief that it has no place in the pristine wilderness. Nothing is more disappointing than finding fragments of it polluting the wilderness. The concept of scout cooking is to make do with natural alternatives – a good scout or guide can always manage without. Most of the materials we will use for this cooking are, by contrast, quick-growing shoots that can be harvested from thickets, particularly in wet areas, and will be swiftly regenerated. Indeed, our impact will be far less significant than that of browsing deer or moose.

In terms of equipment, a small sheath knife is ideal and much safer to use than a folding knife. My own preference is to use a Sami *leuku* for this type of cooking, for its lightness, speed, efficiency and superb performance when splitting firewood. I also carry with me a small bar of pine tar soap so that I can maintain a good standard of hygiene – any fool can be grubby. A miniature bar can easily be carried in the pocket in a tobacco pouch.

FLAVOURED SALT

In remote communities, salt was an essential ingredient for cooking and the preservation of meat and fish. While in scout cooking our options are limited, we can gain a culinary advantage by carrying flavoured salt. There is also no reason why you cannot incorporate black pepper as well to simplify the ingredients you carry.

My preference is fine-quality sea salt, which can be enhanced with the addition of herbs. Combine the ingredients in the ratio of two parts salt to one part flavouring. Grind the dried ingredients with the salt in a coffee grinder.

HUNTER'S SALT
Combine dried juniper berries and dried wild thyme with the salt. This is exceptional when added to wild game or red meat, but also goes well with fish.

ANGLER'S SALT
Combine the zest from lemons, limes and oranges with the salt. This is a superb seasoning for fish dishes but also works well with wild game. It makes a wonderful brine for basting fish.

MARINER'S SALT
Combine dried seaweed with the salt. A really versatile seasoning agent, this is also commercially available.

EMBERS

The most basic and perhaps most ancient human cooking technique is simply to place food in the fire itself. However, as I am sure our early ancestors would have quickly learned, food placed directly into flames is consumed there. To cook in a fire therefore requires a good bed of embers, made from hardwood coals. The food is cooked on or in the embers – the original barbecue. This method suits robust food types or foods that can be cooked in their own skins; delicate foods are apt to break and are difficult to handle.

To cook with embers requires some forethought: embers are best produced from dry, dense firewood. Although by no means essential, a good way to ensure a long-lasting ember bed is to create an ember pit. This can only be done in soil that is of mineral soil or sand and thereby incombustible.

Do not dig an ember pit in soils with a high organic content, such as peat, which may ignite.

To create the pit, simply scrape a hole in the ground. Mostly, this need only be a shallow scrape, although when cooking in quantity or in cold weather, it can be made deeper. You then need to burn a fire over the pit so that it fills with embers and set to cooking your food.

STEAK IN EMBERS

Steak is wonderful when it's cooked on a bed of hardwood embers. To do this, you will need large coals from very dry hardwood, not small ashy coals which will tend to stick to the meat.

1 Create a bed of embers roughly three times the size of the steak. An ember pit is best here.
2 Salt the steak on both sides, then place it on the embers to seal and sear each side.
3 After a few minutes, turn the steak onto a fresh area of coals.
4 Continue turning until the steak is cooked to your liking (see page 258). If the coals cool, they can be refreshed by fanning them with your hat.

BROILING STICK

Broiling sticks are a great way to cook over a bed of embers. They are actually quite elaborate, so usually find their use in woodcraft camps, where their value lies as much in the skill of their manufacture as in their function in cooking. Fashioned from flexible young saplings, they are suspended just above a bed of glowing embers. They are not intended to be held over the fire, as is often the mistaken belief.

EGGS IN EMBERS

The egg is a marvel of nature: nutritious and delicious, it also comes prepacked for scout cooking.

1 The simplest way to cook an egg is to place it in the embers at the edge of the fire. However, it must first be pierced otherwise it will explode, scattering molten egg on anyone who is sitting nearby. To pierce the egg, use the very tip of your knife and peck a hole 1cm (½ in) in diameter in the egg's broadest end.
2 This having been done, take a small stick of green wood and ensure that the egg membrane inside the egg is also well pierced. Alternatively, the egg can be stirred inside the shell with this stick, and you can even insert some finely chopped fresh thyme or rosemary and mix it in.
3 Once the egg has been prepared, settle it into the embers at the edge of the fire with the opening upwards and cook until the contents are done to your liking. Test with a fresh, clean wood sliver.

Beware: left too long, eggs cooked in this way will burn. You should also note that the egg will be very hot when raked from the embers and needs to be allowed to cool before being handled.

BIVALVES

Clams, mussels, razor shells, cockles ... all are delicious bivalves that can easily be cooked under a bed of embers. Here is an Australian aboriginal method:

1 Build a good fire of dry driftwood on the beach.

2 Alongside the fire, flatten an area of sand smooth and large enough for the quantity of bivalves you have to cook.

3 Check that the bivalves are alive by squeezing the edge of the shell; healthy clams will remain shut tight.

4 Place them on the sand with the hinge pointing upwards. Arrange them in this way in neat rows, one row supporting the next.

5 Once ready and embers are available from the fire, using a stick, rake a bed of embers over the bivalves.

6 With good embers, they will only need to cook for a few minutes. Larger, more meaty species, will require longer cooking.

7 Once they are done, rake the embers off the bivalves. You will find that the shells will have opened and that the meat will have shrunk upwards towards the hinge, away from the sand.

OYSTERS

Oysters can be cooked directly on a bed of embers. Lay them with the flatter shell half uppermost. Quick cooking is the order of the day, the oysters cooking in their own juices. Once again, the fire will open the shells – a far safer option in remote country than using a knife to prise them open.

LIMPETS

Limpets are the most overlooked source of food to be found on the coastline. The old English cooking method is my favourite:

1 Collect a good meal of limpets, then find a large, flat rock and place the limpets on the rock, just as you find them naturally.
2 Over the top of this limpet-covered rock ignite a quick, hot fire of dry grass, dry umbellifer stems or snap wood twigs.
3 This flash fire will only last a couple of minutes, after which the ashes can be fanned away and the shells can be lifted away from the cooked limpets.
4 Remove and discard the black blister from the top of the limpets before eating the orange foot. They are a little rubbery, but were once an important food of our forebears and are extremely nutritious.

BURDOCK, CATTAIL AND POTATO

Some vegetables can also be quickly cooked in embers. Classic survival foods include the root of wild burdock and the rhizome of greater reedmace. Both of these roots can be cooked directly in their natural skins.

Burdock roots that have been harvested in spring are the best ones for cooking in this way as the root starches convert to sweet sugars over winter. Simply cook the root in the embers at the edge of a campfire. The rind of the root is about 4mm (⅛in) thick and once cooked, can simply be peeled away.

Greater reedmace rhizomes, which are protected by a spongy outer layer, can actually be cooked in the flames of the fire, although embers are better. I cook them until they are charred all over, but not brittle. Having been removed from the fire and allowed to cool to the point at which they can be handled, the starchy fibres in the middle of the rhizome can be pulled out with your front teeth and the edible starch sucked from the stingy fibres, which are then discarded.

Potatoes are a wonderful food to cook in embers. The secret is to 1) have a sufficient depth of embers to cook them – an ember pit is ideal; and 2) protect the outside of the potato from scorching by coating it in damp clay or wrapping it in large leaves, such as burdock or butterbur. These things having been done, simply bury the potatoes in the embers an hour before the meal is to be served. Dig them out after 45–60 minutes of cooking and break open the clay or leaf wrapper. Timings will vary according to the weather and season. A skewer can be used to probe the potatoes to establish their doneness.

DAMPER

Damper is the original bread, and was historically made from wild grass seeds. I have had the privilege to assist Australian Aboriginals gathering, yandying (agitating the seed to separate the seeds from the chaff) and grinding wild grass seeds to cook a heavy, incredibly filling, nutritious damper in the ashes of a mulga wood fire. It is a memory that I recall fondly every time I cook bread outdoors, for in many ways that was the original bread-baking process. Today, damper is made in a very similar way but with convenient, store-bought white flour, which is far less nutritious than the wild original.

INGREDIENTS

Makes 1 loaf

2 cups (250g) plain
  flour
2 tsp baking powder
½ tsp salt
about ⅔ cup (175ml)
  warm water

METHOD

1 Make a fire to produce a really good bed of hardwood embers. Lay the fire on a smooth, flat piece of ground. Once the fire has produced sufficient embers, rake these aside, leaving a thin layer of ash.

2 Meanwhile, mix the dry ingredients well and form into a dough by adding warm water little by little until a smooth, fairly dry dough is formed. You may not need all the water, or you may need a drop more.

3 Only a light kneading is required as the rise in this bread comes from the gas produced by the baking powder. Form the dough into a ball and flatten it into a loaf shape about thumb-thickness high.

4 Move the burning sticks of the fire to one side, then rake back the embers and some of the ash.

5 Place the bread directly on top of the remaining hot ashes. Rake back the removed ashes, cover the bread and now cover over with the embers previously moved.

6 The damper will take 30–40 minutes to bake. Cooking times will vary according to the size of the damper, the moistness of the dough and the heat of the fire. Once done, it will resonate with a deep tone when tapped. You can also use a skewer to test the damper; when cooked, the skewer will emerge from the damper dry.

7 Remove the damper from the ashes and brush off any ash before serving warm.

MOSS, SEAWEED AND LEAVES

STEAMED IN MOSS

Sphagnum moss, the amazing peat moss, has many wonderful attributes that those versed in bushcraft can take advantage of. In many of the northern wildernesses it is also infinitely available. It can be used to quickly steam fish or other foods. Simply place a layer of moss directly onto a hearty campfire, place the food to be cooked onto the moss and then cover with another layer of moss. The food will steam nicely. Fish may need to be turned during the steaming. This is a great way to cook eggs, which do not need to be pierced (unlike when cooking in embers). They will pop when the eggs crack, but the energy is contained by the moss so they don't explode everywhere. If you prefer, the eggs can of course be pierced to keep them more intact (see page 55).

BULL KELP BAGS

In New Zealand there is a variety of bull kelp that can be split open to form a bag that's ideal for cooking, storing and transporting food – all uses that the local Maori put it to. Cut the kelp 40–60cm (16–24in) from the broad tip and carefully work your hand into the cut end, like putting your hand into a sock. Stuff the bag thus created with the food to be cooked and tie the bag shut with a strip of seaweed. Pop the bag in the embers of a fire to steam the food.

SEA BASS STEAMED WITH WILD FENNEL AND SEAWEED

Seaweed can be used in the same way as moss to make an impromptu steamer and can lend an ocean aroma to the food. Classically, this method is used to steam shellfish or fish. Sea bass is especially wonderful cooked in this way.

1 First, you will need a fairly robust fire. If using driftwood, avoid wood that is polluted with oil or the food will be tainted and ruined.
2 Place a layer of seaweed on the fire, then lay a bed of wild fennel leaves onto the seaweed, followed by the fish, then more fennel and, finally, more seaweed.
3 Turn the fish once during cooking. It is done when the flesh is opaque and flakes easily when probed with the tip of a knife.

LEAFY BRANCHES

In the same way that moss can be used to steam eggs, sprays of leaves from alder, birch, willow, sycamore, oak, hazel or rowan can be used, particularly for steaming fish. Place a thick layer of branches that are verdant with fresh leaves on the fire, then place the fish on top, followed by another layer of leafy branches. If the leaves are dry, soak them before use. Should they show any signs of combusting, sprinkle them with some water.

WRAPPED IN LEAVES

Cooking in leaves conjures images of neat packages of wild boar wrapped in banana leaves or palm fronds being carefully placed in a tropical ground oven and we shall indeed consider the ground oven (see pages 249–56). But for the purposes of smaller-scale trail cooking, leaves can be used immediately. Indeed, leaves are the aluminium foil of the bush, except that they are infinitely renewable, totally organic and naturally return to the soil.

Many large enveloping leaves can be used for cooking, the key factor being that they are not toxic. Here, some homework will be required for the part of the world you are exploring. If large leaves are not available, the food may be cut into smaller portions to suit more modest-sized leaves, such as sycamore or wild flax. Leaf cooking on embers is mostly used for the more delicate fish or meats.

CHICKEN WITH LEMON IN DOCK LEAVES

Although more elaborate than is usual when scout cooking, this recipe is a great way into this style of trail cooking.

1 Collect some large dock leaves – look for clean, healthy leaves. Wash the leaves if necessary, particularly if they have been gathered near to livestock or human occupation. You will also need some string; butcher's twine can be used or you can do as I do and strip out some stringy fibres from stinging nettle stems or some straps of bark from a willow shoot.

2 Build a modest trail fire over a small ember pit. While the embers are forming, slice a chicken breast into pieces that suit the size of the leaves you have.

3 Place the chicken on two dock leaves, then add a couple of slices of lemon and a squeeze of lemon juice, a knob of butter, some ground black pepper and a pinch of salt.

4 Fold the leaves around the chicken and add more as necessary so that all the edges are sealed. Tie the bundle neatly with string.

5 When the embers have formed, bury the leaf package in them and cook the chicken for 30 minutes.

6 Rake the package carefully from the embers as the string may have burned through, then carefully open and check that the chicken is cooked; the juices should run clear and the flesh should be opaque. If it isn't, close the package as best you can and return it to the embers for a few more minutes.

VARIATION

You can try substituting the lemon with garlic.

RABBIT IN BURDOCK WITH WILD WATER MINT

This is more of a pure scout recipe than the chicken one, for times when we are unlikely to have anything more with us than some salt.

1 Debone the rabbit portions and wrap them in wild burdock leaves.
2 Add some sprigs of freshly gathered wild water mint and a sprinkle of salt. In the spring, I also add peppery lady's smock leaves and any other wild spring greens I can forage, such as lesser stitchwort, cleavers and chickweed.
3 Wrap and tie as described for the chicken recipe (see page 62) and cook in the same way.

VARIATIONS

■ Wild hedge garlic and ramson flowers can be used instead of the mint, but go easy with wild garlic flavours as they can overpower the main ingredient.
■ Eel is an amazing wild food that reaches dizzy heights when cooked in leaves as the gelatinous fats are retained. Follow the same method as for rabbit.

STICKY RICE IN A BAMBOO TUBE

When I am travelling in the rainforest with an abundance of bamboo, this is my go-to method for cooking sticky rice. A second tube loaded with freshwater shrimps and some slices of wild ginger and the whole meal is complete.

1 Soak some sticky rice in water for at least 4 hours.
2 Meanwhile, cut out a section of fresh green bamboo 5–10cm (2–4in) in diameter, then section the tube so that one node will form the base. At the opening, you can either cut below the next node or above it, then pierce the node to create an opening.
3 Drain the sticky rice, then use it to fill the opening. Plug the tube's open end with a wad of banana leaf.
4 Prop the tube at an angle over the fire and rotate at least once during the cooking time – about 30 minutes.
5 Remove the tube from the fire, split it with a *parang* (machete) and peel in two so you can eat the rice directly from the tube.

To prevent the pressure of the steam from forcing rice out of the tube, cut two opposing slits just below the lip of the cooking tube. Then place a flat strip of bamboo through these slits, across the mouth of the tube.

VARIATION

The more refined method is to line the tube with a rolled rectangle of banana leaf. This is filled with the pre-soaked rice and plugged with a banana leaf. The tube is also cooked at an angle over the fire and turned. When cooked, the tube is split open to reveal the long cylinder of cooked rice wrapped in the banana leaf. This wrapping can be left on and the cylinder sliced to appropriate-sized portions.

SKEWERS

Cooking food on a sharpened stick seems such an obvious way to cook, but to do it right requires a little more skill and patience than is apparent at first glance. Legion are the young campers who have discovered that when you get it wrong, the result is food burned crispy black on the outside and not cooked at all on the inside. An equally large number of people have watched aghast as a perfectly cooked sausage slides from the skewer into the furnace of the fire. As with most things in bushcraft, there is a right way, with the secret lying in the details.

The first thing is to choose a type of wood that is non-toxic and preferably won't impart

any flavour to the meat. Hazel, birch and willow are three good choices here. Select nice straight shoots wherever possible. The wood should be green; if dead wood must be used, the wood will need to be soaked for at least 1 hour first.

The bark should be sliced away from the stick where it will be in contact with the food and a point should be put on the skewer. At its simplest, that is all that needs to be done. However, a round skewer has a disadvantage: the food will tend to rotate around the stick, making it difficult to turn and cook evenly. What's worse, chasing food that is rotating around the stick will lead to its loosening and increase the chance of it being lost in the fire. It's therefore better to give the skewer a more angular cross section – roughly triangular for some foods and more diamond-shaped for others.

With all skewer cooking, the heat comes from the side of the fire, not from the flames, so arrange the skewers so that they sit at an angle to the fire, preferably stuck into the ground (sharpen the butt end for this purpose) or wedged between rocks or logs. If it is windy, place the skewers so that the fire's heat is blowing onto them. Rotate the skewers occasionally, being careful not to be scalded by hot liquid or fat dripping down the skewer from the cooking food.

Skewers can be reused several times so long as they are sterilised in the flames between use.

If introducing youngsters to this method, do not let them ignite the ends of the sticks and wave them around like sparklers; eyes are too easily damaged by this tomfoolery. Also, never leave skewers planted standing upright in the soil or snow since if you bend over in the dark it is all too easy to impale your face on a skewer.

STICKY EGG

This is a great way to cook an egg when there is snow on the ground and reliable embers are more difficult to produce.

1 For this method, the skewer should be round in cross section, with a gentle taper. This makes for a better fit so the egg will adhere to the skewer better, enabling it to be rotated.

2 Pierce the egg at both ends by carefully pecking with the point of your knife. The larger hole will be at the broad end of the egg and should match the diameter of the thick part of the skewer taper. At the other end, the egg need only be pierced with a 5mm (¼in) hole.

3 Carefully thread the egg onto the skewer and arrange it over the fire. As soon as any egg white weeping from the holes is heated it will coagulate and seal the package.

4 Cook gently until the egg is done. The skewer's positioning, the weather and the heat of the fire will determine the cooking speed, so use your best judgement.

SKEWERED APPLE

An apple cooked on a skewer is wonderful fare on a cold day. Use a skewer with a triangular cross section. Slice the apple through its equator, skewer from the flat side, then cook gently, skin towards the fire. When the apple is cooked the skin will slide off easily.

SKEWERED SAUSAGES

Sausages are made for skewer cooking. The conventional British sausage, the beloved 'banger', is usually skewered through its length, one sausage per stick being the normal way and two per stick being the maximum.

1 Shave the skewer to a triangular cross-section. If you intend to cook more sausages, skewer them with a suitably forked skewer stuck through the side. This can be left round as rotation will not be an issue. Thick-skinned sausages can be cooked on round cross-section kebab sticks. Slice the skin to allow for the meat expanding.

2 Once skewered, the secret to cooking sausages is to do so slowly, at the edge of the fire, so that they are properly cooked through. Never rush the proceedings or, despite looking delicious on the outside, they will be raw in the middle.

3 Cut one sausage open to ensure it is completely cooked through. If cooking after dark, use a head torch to do this. If you can't be completely confident about the meat itself, this checking process is even more important. Once, many years ago in Central Africa, fellow travellers and I purchased kebabbed goat from a local market. I took the precaution of inspecting the meat before consuming it – something my colleagues derided me for – but they soon stopped laughing when they discovered that one of their half-eaten kebabs was green inside with decay...

VARIATION

Once a single sausage on a stick has been properly cooked it can be coated in a thin layer of twist dough (see pages 74–5) and further cooked until the bread is baked. Et voilà! The backwoods hot dog.

BRIGAND STEAK

On canoe trips, I like to carry along a salami or similar Bologna sausage. While this may be sliced and eaten cold, it is can also be dramatically transformed with the addition of fire. Served with bannock, this is the canoe trip equivalent of a burger.

1 Slice sufficient sausage into discs and kebab them onto a carefully shaved triangular skewer. If you have onion, mushroom, pepper or tomato, intersperse slices of these between the sausage discs.
2 Cook beside the fire until golden.

ROBIN HOOD'S VENISON STEAK

This is a wonderful hunter's delicacy. While any good cut of steak can be used, a generous chunk of back steak is superlative.

1 Carve a sword-like skewer with a diamond cross section and use it to pierce the steak.
2 Cook the steak carefully beside the fire until it is done to your preference.
3 Season with a sprinkle of salt and pepper if you have it.

SKEWERED FISH

The simplest and quickest way of all to cook a fish you have caught is to skewer it. At its most basic, this involves gutting the fish, then passing a skewer from mouth to tail and propping it beside the fire to cook. The lucky angler can easily adapt this method to cook many fish.

1   Prepare a small, flat skewer, diamond in cross section, for each fish you have to cook, putting points on both ends. Prepare a fire that's long enough to accommodate all of the fish you wish to cook.
2   Descale the fish, cut out the gills, slice along the belly and remove the entrails.
3   Cutting as necessary, skewer the fish from tail to mouth, with the skewer close to the spine for support. Slice the skin of the fish with many small cuts.
4   Set the skewers into the ground, angled towards the fire. Cook the fish on the thicker back side first, turning to finish the belly side.
5   Throughout the cooking, baste the fish with a brine solution made by dissolving 1 tbsp salt in 1 cup (250ml) water (or make up a greater quantity using the same ratio). You can also add 1 tsp sugar to the solution if you have it. Angler's salt (see page 52) is wonderful in this recipe.

SKEWERED CRAYFISH

Crayfish, langoustine or lobster can all be skewered and cooked on the fire, and are delicious.

1   Kill the shellfish by cutting across the spinal cord at the head. Remove the stomach thread by carefully wiggling loose the central tail fin and pulling slowly; the alimentary canal, which looks like a black thread, should pull free.
2   In the same passage, skewer the shellfish with a suitable-sized skewer, triangular in cross section if possible and pointed at both ends.
3   Plant the skewer in the ground on the hot side of the fire, angled towards the fire. As the shellfish cooks, it will turn scarlet.

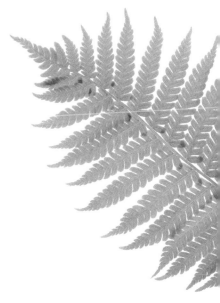

SOME MORE, SOME MORE... MARSHMALLOW S'MORES

First described in *Tramping and Trailing with the Girl Scouts* in 1927, this has since become the classic childhood delight of Canadian and American camping. These are also, strangely, loved by some of the world's best and most gnarly canoeists. Mentioning no names here...

1 Using the most rudimentary of skewers – even just a broken bendy twig – cook a large marshmallow over the fire. Should it catch, lightly blow it out.
2 Once cooked to your liking, add it to a digestive biscuit or other sickly-sweet cookie, top with chocolate of any description – from bar chocolate to the rather more 'sophisticated' chocolate spread – then top like a sandwich with another cookie and enjoy.

Be careful to warn children that the molten marshmallow will burn, should they get it on their skin.

CAMPFIRE BREAD

This is a widely used method of cooking, particularly popular among the First Nations in Canada, where it is a popular part of the seasonal goose feast Sikipwân. While a damper normally requires dry, warm ground for the cooking, this method can be used when the ground is damp or still covered in snow.

INGREDIENTS

Makes 2 loaves

2 cups (250g) plain flour
2 tsp baking powder
1 tsp salt
about ⅔ cup (175ml) water, preferably warm

METHOD

1 Take a green stick of a non-toxic wood such as birch. If possible, look for a stick that's 5cm (2in) thick. If this is not possible, use a stick of thumb thickness. Point one end of the stick so that it can be pushed into the ground or snow. Shave off the bark for the top 30–40cm (12–16in) of the stick.
2 Mix the dry ingredients well and form into a dough by adding warm water little by little until a smooth, fairly dry dough forms. You may not need all the water, or you may need a drop more. The water can be added cold but better results are achieved with warm water.
3 Only a light kneading is required, just to bring the dough together. Form the dough into a ball and flatten into a flat loaf shape about thumb thickness high.
4 If using the thick stick, heat over the fire to scorching point and then form the dough over the end, wrapping it down the sides. If using a thin

stick, heat to scorching point and roll a long thin sausage of dough between your palms. Wrap the sausage spiral fashion around the stick, leaving a small finger-wide gap between the turns of the spiral. You can also wrap a cooked sausage in this manner (see page 69).

5 Plant the stick so that it is tilted towards the heat at the side of the fire. Rotate the stick as necessary to cook the dough evenly.

6 Serve with butter and jam or with fat collected from meat or fish that's also cooking over the fire.

HOOK SUSPENSION

Suspending food beside a fire or a wood-burning stove, particularly inside a tent, is a classic northwoods way of cooking found throughout the boreal forest. The suspension can be with a specially shaped vertical prop, with a cord and skewer, or a hook from above. By this means, one fire can be used to cook many items. A typical example was the roasting of a caribou head beside the coals of a fire, caribou nose being a delicacy among the northern tribes in Canada.

CARIBOU RIBS

Caribou ribs were the classic hunter's treat across the boreal forest. They were cooked beside the fire, suspended on a vertical prop carved with a point and a notch to prevent the ribs sliding down the prop.

To do this yourself, cook from the inner rib side first as the hot bones will help to cook the meat evenly, then turn to complete the cooking from the outer side. Season with salt to taste. Usually, the ribs are accompanied by black tea and sometimes bannock, in which case, some of the dripping fat should be added to the bannock mix.

LEG OF VENISON

A shoulder of venison can be suspended on a wooden hook hung from a tent frame beside the wood-burning stove. Given the occasional spin, this method roasts the shoulder slowly and evenly. In an arctic winter camp, a shoulder is often set up in this way in a tent in the morning and is cooked slowly so that it is available to those returning to the tent after checking fish nets.

BANNOCK

In the tent of a winter camp in northern Canada there is a constant demand for bannock. The resulting production line involves starting the bannock atop the wood-burning stove and, once of sufficient body, it is finished on a prop stick beside the wood-burning stove, freeing the stove top for starting the next bannock.

GOOSE OR DUCK

The goose hunt is an important northern tradition; a successful hunt results in a Sikipwân feast. For this, the geese are prepared by plucking and drawing the entrails, the belly cavity is stitched closed with a twig, the wing bones are tied to the side of the carcass and the legs are skewered in position. The carcass is then suspended beside a fire either inside a tent or outside, utilising a windbreak to ensure good cooking warmth. Beneath the goose, a pan is set to collect the dripping fat to both prevent wastage and out of respect to the bird; respect for their prey is of paramount importance to the elders of the northern First Nations.

The geese are spun to be cooked rotisserie style and are basted with the fat collected in the pan. Near the end of the cooking time, Campfire Bread (see pages 74–5) is also cooked beside the fire to be eaten with the meat.

Sometimes, a special fireplace is made inside the cooking tent with a wooden frame filled with beach sand so that the twist sticks can easily be set up when needed.

CLEFT STICK

Cleft stick cooking opens up greater potential for cooking heavier foods, since the method provides greater stability.

TROUT

Trout cooked beside a fire are delicious. They can easily be cooked by filleting out the bones in a similar way to that described opposite for salmon or char, except that for trout, you sever the spine so that the tail section is left on. The fish is then spread open with the aid of only one cross-skewer, which passes through a split in the support stick, as shown. Measure the support stick to size and make the split first. I like to widen one side of the split to allow the cross-skewer to be easily located. Point the end of the cross-skewer like a sharp screwdriver to easily pass into the split.

SPLIT-STICK SALMON

Done properly, this is a divine way to cook fish such as salmon, char, large trout or lake trout. In my opinion, it cannot be bested by dishes served at even the most acclaimed restaurant.

1 Begin by selecting a suitable-sized cleft stick for your fish. A willow shoot is ideal for this. Remove the bark and strip it into straps, which will be used later to secure the cleft stick. Carve the necessary cross-skewers. Now prepare the fish.

2 Open the belly from the anal vent and remove the entrails. Next, fillet the fish – this is easily

done for salmonids. Remove the dorsal and pelvic fins, then cut down to the spine behind the gills but not through the spine.

3 With the point of your knife, continue this cut either side of the spine to exit at the belly behind the pectoral fins. Now slowly run your thumb along either side of the spine, gently easing out the ribs from the flesh. Continue all the way to the tail and then cut around the skin at the tail so that the spine comes away with all of the ribs, the head and the tail attached. Do not worry about leaving some meat on the ribs as they will be used to make Salmon Soup (see page 172).

4 Depending on the size of the fish, you will need either two skewers for average-sized fish or three for large fish. Fish skin is very tough,

so make holes for the skewers with the tip of your knife. Insert the skewers from the flesh side so that they pass largely over the skin surface.

5 With the skewers positioned, place the whole spread fillet in the cleft stick with the widest end at the top. Bind the cleft stick closed with the willow strips. If necessary, bind below the split as well for support.

6 The cleft stick can now be set at an angle towards the fire. It is best to first make a hole for this purpose with a sharp stake hammered in with an axe.

7 Ideally using an alder wood fire, cook the salmon until it is crispy and golden, then turn to complete the cooking on the skin side. Never turn the fish back or flesh may drop from the skin.

HUNTER'S SPATCHCOCK POUSSIN WITH HONEY GLAZE

This is a classic hunter's way to cook a small fowl on the trail. A meal cooked quickly, without the need for or fuss of utensils or cooking paraphernalia, it epitomises the freedom and self-reliance of outdoor life.

The process can be scaled up for larger birds, but that rather breaks the spirit of the method, as larger birds require a larger fire and longer cooking time – things that are more appropriate to the fixed camp.

In its simplest form, the meat is cooked without a glaze, perhaps sprinkled with a pinch of hunter's salt (see page 52) once cooked. But if you have some honey, the dish can be elevated to a higher plane. Without honey, maple syrup can be used, or if you are a hundred miles from civilisation with no alternative, brown sugar heated with a little water may be substituted.

Although the method appears simple it is not lacking in skill. The secret is to cook over the clean heat of embers and to honour the ingredients by not rushing the cooking. Also, do not leave the meat over the fire after the cooking is completed; the dish should be tender and succulent, not dry and stringy.

1 Begin by kindling a small lunch fire. Choose dry hardwood fuel to produce a good bed of embers. While the wood burns to embers, swing a billycan over the flames for hot water. This is not just for tea; we shall need hot water to clean our hands and knife after preparing the fowl for cooking.

2 Next, prepare the tongs used to grasp food over the fire like giant tweezers. For these, choose wood that splits well and that can provide a bark that can be used for cord to tie the tong firmly shut. Ideal woods are willow or sweet chestnut. Hazel is also excellent, but the bark cannot be used for binding.

3 Spatchcock the bird using the method with the legs tucked under the skin. To spatchcock a fowl, cut straight through the backbone and flatten the carcass. This can be done easily by simply pressing down, although there are two tendons which if cut make the process much easier. Remove the wing tips at the first joint and do the same for the feet. Using two skewers spread the carcass so that it will cook evenly. Secure the spatchcocked fowl in the split stick by binding the split shut with bark strips, stinging nettle fibres or other suitable string, such as well-soaked kitchen twine.

4 Start the cooking over the hot embers with the bony side of the spatchcocked bird towards the fire, and as the embers cool, lower the meat closer to the embers and rotate to cook the fleshy side. Slow, gentle cooking is the secret to success. Cooking times vary according to the firewood and weather; in most cases, 1 hour is sufficient for a poussin. As always, check that the juices run clear and that the meat is completely opaque.

5 During the cooking, baste the outside of the skin with honey, which will make the skin shiny and mouth-wateringly gorgeous.

6 Remove the bird from the heat and allow it to rest for a few minutes. Serve on a bed of clean fresh leaves, underside up.

HOT ROCKS

Heated rocks can be used in a variety of ways for cooking. One of the strangest I have seen was in Mongolia, where a goat was slaughtered, cleaned and boned out entirely through the neck and then the resulting carcass was filled with red-hot rocks and sealed. The goat was then simultaneously cooked externally over embers.

I have also cooked birds with the feathers on, opened and gutted and the body cavity filled with two suitably sized red-hot rocks. The whole thing is then wrapped up and carried in a rucksack for several hours until cooked.

More practically, however, hot rocks can be made into a hot plate by either directly heating them from underneath or by creating a pavement of suitable flat rocks on the ground and burning a hot fire atop them for long enough to charge the pavement with sufficient heat for cooking. Both methods work well: the pavement method suits cooking for a large group and the direct heating method can be quick and expedient, so long as the flat rock used as the hot plate is thick enough to resist the heating, but not so thick that it takes too long to heat.

Whenever heating rocks, care must be exercised in the choice of rock used. Rocks such as flint, which may naturally contain air pockets, are apt to explode, as will rocks gathered from wet places or stream beds. This is because the moisture expanding faster than it can be shed from the rock leads to an explosive build-up of pressure. Rocks for heating therefore need to be sedimentary in nature, and dry. Also, they should be heated gradually. Do not underestimate the danger of an exploding rock. I once witnessed a 1.8m (6ft) long, 40cm (15in)-diameter oak log thrown 1.8m (6ft) by such an explosion. Never use concrete or bricks for cooking for the same reason.

When cooking on a hot rock it is a good idea to improvise a brush to sweep away dry, gritty particles from the rock surface and to use some fat or oil to cook with. Mushrooms and grouse breasts are delightful cooked on a hot rock together.

If you wish to be more creative with a hot rock, try cooking chicken fajita ingredients – chicken breast strips, onion chopped into rings, red and green peppers, red chilli pieces, a squeeze of lime juice and a splash of tabasco or Maggi sauce. Serve in rock-warmed tortillas with guacamole and sour cream.

For more on this cooking method, see also page 90.

PLANKING

Of all the scout cooking techniques, planking is perhaps the most delicate of all, while remaining flavourful. At a casual glance it would appear that the food will be dry and taste heavily of smoke, but in fact nothing is further from the truth: planking cooks the food in the radiant heat to the side of the fire, seals the surface quickly and preserves the moisture. The food takes on the lightest smoking and is subtly perfumed by the aromas rising from the planking board itself. Not surprisingly, this method is a favourite for cooking fish and is still widely used in wilderness camps across Scandinavia.

All manner of foods can be planked, the only prerequisite being that they are thin in nature. Popular foods are bacon, salmon and trout fillets. The plank can be used multiple times, simply being sterilised on the fire for

a few moments before reuse. Breads can even be planked if the dough is made so that it is thin and sticky enough to adhere to the plank without the need for pins.

For the plank, choose a suitable-sized log of dry, non-toxic wood. If possible, try to avoid resinous woods. My favourite wood choices are alder and pussy willow, which lend a sweet aroma to the food. Split the log with an axe into two neat halves and you have two planks ready to go. If you wet the wood before use, it will supply more aroma during cooking; how much you wet it depends on the wood and the conditions, so let experience be your guide.

The pins must be made from a non-toxic wood that's harder in nature than the board. Look for hard, naturally seasoned wood. Split a piece down to a splint roughly 10 x 7 x 300mm (²⁄₅ x ¼ x 12in). Carve this into small wedge-shaped pins as shown.

PLANK-COOKED FISH

This is a stable and reliable cooking method, which is easy to watch while preparing other ingredients. Once cooked, the fish can be cut into portions and served on plates or simply eaten from the board in the time-honoured woods way.

1 Lay the fish fillet on the board skin side down and pierce the fish where the pins will be located. This is essential as the skin is very tough. With the poll of your axe, hammer the pins into the plank with their edges in line with the grain. Four pins usually suffice.
2 Season the flesh with salt and ground black pepper. In a fishing camp, bring salt mixed with dry seaweed for this if you can – it is quite delicious.
3 Prop the plank beside the fire with the aid of a forked stick, a rock or a convenient log. Place the plank on the downwind side of the fire.
4 Cook gently beside the fire, turning the plank as necessary.

JOHNNY CAKE, OR HOE CAKE

During the American Civil War, Confederate soldiers made a version of the 'Johnny Cake', which they called 'Sloosh' or 'Ramrod Rolls'. For this, they stirred cornmeal into bacon grease and added water to make the dough, adding an egg too, if it was available. The resulting dough was fried on any available implement – even shovels – or wrapped as a twist around a ramrod or stick and cooked over a fire.

INGREDIENTS

1 cup (150g) cornmeal
½ tsp salt
1 tsp sugar or sweetener (demerara, brown, maple syrup or molasses)
1 cup (250ml) boiling water
½ cup edible wild berries or nuts, optional

METHOD

1 Mix together the cornmeal, salt and sugar or sweetener, then add the boiling water and stir in.
2 Allow the cornmeal to absorb the liquid for 10 minutes.
3 If you have edible wild berries or nuts to hand, these can be added now. If the mixture is very stiff, add some cold water to relax it. You are looking to create a stiff batter consistency.
4 Heat the cooking board to scorching point beside the fire.
5 Remove the board from the fire and apply the batter, which will stick and should not be more than 1cm (½in) thick.
6 Cook the Johnny Cake by placing the board in the heat beside the fire, tilted appropriately. Turn the board as necessary.

VARIATION

Alternatively, the mixture can be relaxed with water or milk to a consistency slightly thicker than pancake mix and cooked as small pancakes on a griddle or in a frying pan.

ORIGINAL RECIPE FOR JOHNNY CAKE

'Scald 1 pint of milk and put to 3 pints of Indian meal, and half pint of flour—bake before the fire. Or scald with milk two thirds of the Indian meal, or wet two thirds with boiling water, add salt, molasses and shortening, work up with cold water pretty stiff, and bake as above.'

American Cookery, Amelia Simmons (1796)

GRIDDLE AND GRILL

PERHAPS THE TYPE OF OUTDOOR COOKING that we are all most familiar with is grill cooking or, as we call it today, barbecue. The griddle will be more familiar perhaps from short-order dinners – quickly seared steak or fish steaks, and the like. Both methods of cooking are well applied outdoors and are closely related, sharing many basic procedures.

GRIDDLE

Griddle cooking is cooking on a hot surface, akin to using a frying pan, but a little different. The original griddles were made from hot flat stones or stone slabs. These griddles can either be heated prior to the cooking or, in the case of a metal griddle, heated while cooking. On a vehicle-based expedition it is easy to transport a metal griddle with folding legs. I use a simple small griddle-cum-grill. It is only small but perfectly adequate for two people and with organised cooking can serve four, particularly when used in conjunction with other cooking vessels.

The advantage of griddle cooking is that the food is not exposed to flames or flare-ups from fat dripping onto hot embers. It is even possible to cook with a griddle over flames,

although cooking over embers is the preferable method. While in many camps little more than bacon, eggs and sausages will be cooked on a griddle, it can actually be used to cook all manner of foods: fish, shellfish, vegetables, noodles, potatoes and rice all cook beautifully. However, to do so well requires more than average griddle skill. All too often, a griddle is simply dumped on a pile of blazing twigs and bacon and eggs are thrown on to be cooked until nearly blackened. Handled well though, a griddle provides a quick and enjoyable way to cook food healthily. It is a kitchen tool you can easily fall in love with.

In a strange way, the best introduction to cooking on a metal griddle is to cook on a stone one – something we also explore in the Scout Cooking chapter (see pages 51–87).

STONE GRIDDLES

Stone griddles come in two basic designs: the paved griddle and the heated slab. Each has its particular merits, which may recommend it in certain circumstance. As with all rocks that will be heated, the rocks should: 1) not be rocks prone to fracture when heated, such as flints or concrete; and 2) the rock should be dry, since damp rocks can explode when the moisture within them expands under heating. Finally, the rocks should be heated slowly, not cast into an already hot fire, to allow them to heat slowly.

THE PAVED GRIDDLE

Paved griddles were traditionally used to cook fish, at which they excel, but they can be used to cook lots of other foods, too. They are vulnerable to rain, however, so unless protected under a tarp shelter, they are strictly for use in fair weather.

The paved griddle comprises large stones with at least one long, broad, flat surface, or flat slabs that can be laid down on the ground to form a rectangular cooking surface. It is a good idea to settle the stones into the substrate so that 2–3cm (about 1in) is protruding. This will hold the rocks steady and stabilise them. While the food to be cooked on the griddle is being prepared, a brisk fire is ignited over the rocks and kept burning to charge the rocks with heat. Small, thin stones do not suit this method as they will cool too quickly after heating.

When the fire has burned down to embers, they are brushed away, along with any ash. The rocks are very hot, so they must not be touched, and young children must be kept away for their safety. The rocks can now be greased with some fat from a joint or with vegetable oil, and the food is then cooked directly on top of the rocks. You will need some long tongs and a spatula to manage the food and a clean plate or board to move the ingredients to as they finish cooking. While at first the rocks will cook food quickly, they soon settle to a more even cooking temperature.

THE HEATED SLAB GRIDDLE

Although it is increasingly being superseded by circular metal griddles cut from oil drums, the heated slab is a classic cooking technique still widely used around the world. In the high deserts of the American South West, for instance, Hopi girls, by tradition, have to demonstrate their ability to bake a wafer-thin corn piki bread on a heated rock slab before they are eligible for marriage. Still in mountain country, where the geology supplies thin flat slabs of rock, they are hastily made and used to cook game, particularly wild grouse.

The advantage of these griddles is that they can be heated from beneath with a small fire made from the dry twigs of heather or other weather-beaten, high-country shrubs. Such twigs burn hotly, so care must always be taken to prevent setting a heather moor alight with disastrous consequences.

Once hot, a small bottle of oil or a little fat from the game is melted and then the breasts of the bird are quickly cooked whole or in strips. A drop of alcohol from a hip flask is a welcome addition since it can be used to flambé the food for improved flavour.

STEEL GRIDDLES

THE PORTABLE GRIDDLE

These are the griddles upon which culinary excellence can be built. The griddle must be taken care of, however; they often suffer considerably from poor care. For optimum results, the carbon-steel griddle plate should be kept in good order. Do not be afraid to set to with fine emery paper to remove rust spots and to create a very smooth cooking surface. This is then washed and dried before being seasoned by heating and wiping over with a little vegetable oil. Do this with some kitchen paper, using tongs and taking care not to burn yourself. Repeat the process until the surface is brown or blue in colour and the paper remains clean when wiped over the plate. Seasoning the griddle in this manner will help prevent food sticking and preserve the metal.

Other than the griddle itself, griddle cooking is all about preparation, of both the fire and the food. While preparing the food for cooking, set a

above A small steel griddle like this is a wonderful tool to transport in a 4x4, providing both a griddle and grill capability.

fire to produce a good bed of embers. The griddle will be set to one side of the fire, so that the far side of the griddle plate is directly over an even ember bed while the near side of the plate has no embers beneath it. In this way, the plate will heat so that the far side is very hot while the near side is only moderately hot. This will take some practice to master and will need to be fine-tuned to the ambient temperature. Once you've managed to arrange the griddle in this way, you will be able to adjust the cooking temperature by moving the ingredients around the plate.

It is a good idea to parboil vegetables so that they will cook more quickly – as you do for stir-frying – and cut slow-cooking vegetables smaller than the rest so that they all cook in the same amount of time. Place a little cooking oil on the griddle to heat before adding the food. Use the oil sparingly; the advantage of the griddle over the frying pan is that we use far less oil. You will, though, need some butter handy to glaze some ingredients, along with salt and pepper. I also routinely use a splash of soy sauce or balsamic vinegar while griddle cooking.

Move the food with the aid of two metal spatulas, a carving fork or tongs. Do not think of the griddle as a brutal heat to cook a meal quickly; take your time and cook gently, with patience. If your griddle is large enough to allow it, placing a pan lid or cloche over the food that is cooking creates a miniature oven effect that can speed cooking and help prevent ingredients from drying out. During the process, keep the cooking surface clean by scraping it with a metal spatula.

Inattention is a recipe for disaster. The golden rule of griddle cooking is: once the food goes on to the hot plate do not take your eyes off it.

As you will discover, griddle cooking is skilful and all about timing. When one food has been seared and moved to a cooler part of the plate another can be receiving hot, quick cooking. Bringing everything together at the right moment is the art, but for all that it sounds daunting, the griddle is a wonderfully social way to cook outdoors with diners sitting around, tormented by the aromas and appearance of the meal. Even if your timing doesn't work out, they are likely to forgive you. Be prepared to have a laugh while you master the griddle.

MUURIKKA PAN

In recent years, this wonderful campfire cooking pan has become available from Finland. A cross between a wok and a griddle, it is designed to sit over the fire and can be used as a portable griddle. Here again, though, the best result will be achieved with embers rather than flames and the Murrikka pan combines beautifully with an ember pit (see pages 54 and 95). Position the pan directly over a round pit so that the centre becomes very hot and the edges are cooler.

CLEANING THE GRIDDLE

Most of the cleaning is achieved with a spatula. Once cooled, wipe the griddle over with kitchen paper dabbed with vegetable oil and then wipe off any excess with a clean piece of paper. If you feel the need, it can be washed with a soapy sponge, rinsed and dried, and then oiled. Do not let the corners fill up with rancid grease.

GRILL

The grill is most familiar as the barbecue or *hibachi* and so needs little introduction. This popular and delicious way to cook has its origins outdoors. The original grill was made of green wood, perhaps simply green wood sticks placed parallel over a bed of embers supported on a log either side. It is still used today, particularly by indigenous hunters in the remaining tropical rainforests who arrange tall grills over fires to both cook food and to smoke and preserve meat or fish for transporting back to a village. It is easy enough to carry a lightweight mesh grill and to improvise supports from rocks or logs, and not uncommonly in Canada, such grills are found waiting to be used in campsite campfires.

Personally, however, I have never carried a grill, preferring where possible to improvise one from some green-wood saplings. You will see some methods below. You might think that these methods will not survive the cooking, but they do and in many cases can be used more than once. What's more, to my mind these simple wooden grills capture the very essence of grilling, for despite the apparent ferocity of the heat source, grilling succeeds by the most delicate and careful application of that heat to the food ingredients.

MANAGING THE FIRE

At home, barbecuing is achieved either using charcoal or gas, both of which provide even, reliable, sustained heat, with the charcoal providing by far the better flavour. Travelling in the wild, however, wood fire is used to achieve the same results. This is the original barbecue and will provide even better flavour, but will also require extra skill and care in the management of the fire. Just as with griddle cooking, preparation is the key to success.

Firewood and ignition

The firewood is vitally important. First, it must be from a non-toxic species of wood. The wood will need to be very dry and from a species that will produce a bed of hot, long-lasting coals. Oak, beech, mulga and mesquite are but a few examples. Dead wood, still standing or snagged in branches above the ground, will be the best. Split wood will burn fastest, but do not split the wood too small, it needs to produce some decent-sized coals.

Light the fire early and build it up well. Judging the correct moment to begin cooking will come with experience. To the smoke-free side of the fire, rake out a bed of embers. This will need to be deep enough to sustain itself for the duration of the cooking. Embers will be consumed faster than charcoal so the depth of embers needs to be deeper.

As your firewood combusts it will pass through a cycle of combustion during which its temperature will increase, rising to a peak, then gradually cool, unless more embers are added. Adding more firewood will have a cooling effect as it returns the surface of your fire to the beginning of the combustion cycle. Should you need more heat, therefore, take embers from a fire burning to one side.

Aim to start cooking just before the heat reaches its peak so that it is at its most intense as you sear the ingredients. As the fire temperature begins to drop, surf on its back, moving the food around the griddle or grill to fine-tune the temperature of the cooking. It is a dynamic process, especially when we take account of the cooling effect of a cold, breezy day. The worst thing that can happen is that you use too much heat and burn the food. The second worst is running out of heat.

In hot countries, it is normal to create embers and just rely on their sustained warmth. In colder climes, it is more normal to keep a fire burning to one side, which can provide fresh embers as required. To establish the heat of the fire, hold your hand over the embers and count slowly until you can no longer hold your hand there. In time, you will become good at judging the fire's heat in this way. A count of five is usually on the mark for cooking meat and for baking. At this point, you should observe the embers glowing red with a white ash covering developing on their surface.

SEASONING AND GLAZES

I season all of my ingredients prior to placing them on the grill. With meat, it is best to apply salt 15–20 minutes prior to the cooking.

Glazes are a wonderful enhancement to grilled food, even just some honey on its own. When using a glaze, I generally add this after the cooking has progressed to what I judge to be the halfway point. If it is applied too early, there is the high probability that the glaze will char, particularly as the majority of glazes contain some form of sugar.

THE METAL GRILL

Ensure that the bed of embers is of even depth, then place the grill over the embers at a height of 10–15cm (4–6in). As for the griddle, arrange it so that there is a hot side and a moderate heat side, unless your cooking is to be even throughout – for example – when cooking spatchcocked poussin, in which case modify the ember bed to suit. Allow the grill to heat up and brush off any charred remains from previous meals with a brass wire brush.

HOW TO GRILL

The food to be cooked should all have been prepared while the fire is burning to coals so that as soon as the embers are in their optimum condition you are ready to begin cooking.

Start, as always, with the foods that will take the longest to cook and utilise the hot and cold areas of your grill accordingly to achieve perfect results. Fragile foods such as fish should be handled delicately, while thicker cuts of meat will need to be turned continuously. Incidentally, try to avoid really thick steaks as there is a tendency for them to dry out on the surface before the centre reaches the correct temperature. Steaks no greater than 2cm (1in) thick are ideal. Thick steaks can always be beaten out to a more convenient thickness.

If fat dropping from the fire causes a flare-up, move the food to one side. While aromas rising from the coals will help to flavour the cooking, burning fat only taints the food.

IMPROVISED GRILLS

The ember pit

Constructing an ember pit is a great way to extend the longevity of your embers. Dig a pit 30cm (12in) deep by whatever width of fire you will be using, making it round or rectangular as your needs dictate. In and over this, burn your fire so that the pit fills with embers. As with the ground oven, lining the bottom with some rocks helps to maintain a sustained supply of heat output.

Once filled with embers, move the fire to one side and cook over the pit. This works extremely well in conjunction with a broiling stick.

Broiling sticks

Broiling sticks are fashioned from green branches or saplings from non-toxic woods such as hazel, willow or birch. They can be made in many ways, the aim being to create a firm, stable grill. A common misconception is that they are held over the fire; a quicker way to feed the fire with good steak is hard to imagine... They should instead be set up as shown on page 100, supported by sticks, logs or rocks. Obviously, they will only last for a short while, but they serve perfectly for most grilling needs and can be simply returned to nature when finished with.

The forest hibachi and the fan

On street corners throughout Japan, chefs at specialist food stalls still cook on skewers set in perfectly neat rows across long, narrow charcoal braziers called *shichirin*, *konro* or *kanteki*. On these commercial grills, all manner of delicious treats can be found cooking, from yakitori and smoked eel to sweetened rice balls and *hachinoko gohan* (sweet wasp larvae). So popular is this way of cooking that in recent years diners have been opened where the guests can cook for themselves on their own table-top *shichirin*. However good these are, though, they pale into culinary insignificance when compared to the original forest grill that was their inspiration.

All that is needed are a couple of straight thumb-thick green shoots about 1m (3.2ft) long, which can be elevated on short, upright forked sticks. Set the sticks wider than a long, narrow ember pit previously filled with embers, about 10cm (4in) above the embers. Split out some skewers from a green stick and carve flat or triangular as the food demands. They must be longer than the width of the supports.

Soak the sticks to protect them during the cooking process, then load them with your ingredients and place them on the grill. As the cooking progresses, rotate the sticks to ensure even cooking. If you have carved the skewers well, they will remain as you set them and not roll back to their original orientation. As the embers burn down, fan them with a bunch of leaves to increase the heat as your needs require.

PERFECT STEAK

Cooking a steak is not difficult, although it is so often done badly. First, ensure that you are using quality, organic meat. Cooking on the griddle or grill relies on enhancing the natural flavour and texture of the ingredients. Simple as these methods may be, they will brutally unmask any flaws in the ingredients.

INGREDIENTS

steak
olive oil
salt and pepper,
   to taste

METHOD

1 About 20 minutes before you intend to cook, prepare the steak. If the steak is very thick, I would suggest gently beating it out to 2cm (1in) in thickness. On the griddle, you can cook slightly thicker steaks – about 3cm (1½in) in thickness – as it is less drying than the grill.

2 Season the steak with salt and pepper and massage it all over with olive oil.

3 Prepare all of your cooking materials: ensure all tools, ingredients, oil, seasoning, etc are within easy reach so that you will not be distracted. Make a final check on the fire.

4 Begin cooking the steak on the hottest part of griddle or grill, searing the surface.

5 This having been done, move the steak to a cooler part of the griddle or grill and continue more slowly. Turn the steak frequently. Remember, steaks that require the most cooking must be carefully cooked, slowly, on less heat, not blasted with the hottest.

6 Using a thermometer or meat probe, test the steak for its state of doneness (see page 258) and once you reach the desired temperature, hold the steak at that temperature for 3 minutes before removing it from the heat.

7 Transfer to a plate to rest for 5 minutes before serving. There is an art to this, so be self-critical and follow the method until you gain the experience to judge the process by eye.

CHILLI-GLAZED POUSSIN

Quick and easy to cook thoroughly, poussin are the perfect fowl for the novice outdoors cook or for young adventurers keen to improve their outdoor cooking skills. More experienced chefs can equally apply this method to a full-sized chicken, although a longer cooking time will be required, along with more careful attention throughout the process.

INGREDIENTS

Serves 2

1 poussin
1 fresh red chilli
2.5cm (1in) piece of
  fresh root ginger
juice of 1 lime
2 tbsp soy sauce
1 tbsp brown sugar

METHOD

1 Prepare the skewers (see page 95), then soak in clean water for 30 minutes to prevent them from burning.

2 Prepare the fire using good ember-producing hardwood. While the fire burns down, prepare the bird and the glaze.

3 Spatchcock the fowl using the method involving skewers (see page 82).

4 Prepare the glaze. Seed and finely chop the chilli, then peel and finely chop the ginger. Combine and mix with the lime juice, soy sauce and brown sugar.

5 Baste the bird with the glaze and place bony side down on the griddle to cook. Do not allow the meat to burn. If necessary, remove the bird from the griddle and adjust the quantity of embers for a cooler heat.

6 Turn the meat and cook on the fleshy side until the skin is golden brown, basting as necessary.

7 Once the internal temperature is correct when checked with a thermometer or probe (see page 258), remove from the heat and allow to rest before serving.

CHICKEN YAKITORI

Skewer cooking is a favourite Asian cooking method, reaching great delicacy in street markets. Almost any food can be cooked on skewers, broccoli, shrimps, asparagus, meat, fish or shellfish, but whatever the ingredients, all are elevated when cooked in a yakitori glaze.

INGREDIENTS

Serves 2–4

2 chicken breasts
2 leeks
2 red peppers, seeded
6 mushrooms
3 tsp brown sugar
4 tbsp water
½ cup (125ml) soy
  sauce
½ cup (125ml) mirin
1 garlic clove
ground black pepper
  or shichimi pepper
pinch of salt

METHOD

1 Prepare some skewers (see page 95) and soak them in clean water for 30 minutes.
2 Meanwhile, beat the chicken breasts to an even thickness of 1cm (½in). Cut into 3cm (1½in) squares.
3 Cut the leeks into 4cm (2in) segments and the pepper into 3cm (1½in) squares, and trim the stems on the mushrooms.
4 Prepare the skewers, alternately threading on the meat squares and the vegetables.

5 In a small billycan, combine the sugar, water, soy sauce and mirin and heat to dissolve the sugar. While it's heating, crush and add the garlic, and stir in the pepper. Once the sugar has dissolved, set the glaze aside.
6 Begin cooking the skewers. It is traditional to have some skewers simply seasoned with salt as well as those brushed with the sweet glaze.
7 Once the cooking has reached what you consider to be the halfway point, glaze the skewers that will be sweet. Do not worry if the glaze seems thin, it is built up in layers. Season the remaining skewers with a pinch of salt.
8 Continue glazing the sweet skewers little by little until they are cooked, and the glaze is a beautiful glossy brown. Cook the salted skewers until they too are golden. Serve hot.

FRYING

MANY YEARS AGO, I drove through the remote suburbs of Moscow with a remarkably gifted Swedish anthropologist. As we approached a particularly grey, Orwellian tower block, with masses of workers pouring out on their way to their employment, my colleague shrank down in his seat and pulled up his collar, trying desperately to make himself invisible as he muttered '*skavoroda*', '*skavoroda*', in a voice full of fear. Only after much questioning did I discover that he had once had an amorous association with a lady from that dour apartment building, who, eventually tiring of his wandering nature, had chased him out with blows from a *skavoroda*, a frying pan. Whenever I see a frying pan now, I think of him. It is strange how the memory works. Anyway, I dedicate this chapter to his memory.

Frying is an easy and delicious way to cook meat, fish and many vegetables. Done well, the flavours are wonderful, the food retains its moisture and tenderness, and the surface of the dish takes on the allure of a golden sunset.

But to fry well outdoors requires care handling the heat of the pan; our aim is to honour our ingredients, not to scorch them in bitter, burned black oil. I cannot count the number of times I have seen ruined food drowning in black oil. The secret is in the way we manage the heat source. Never fry over a raging fire or you will certainly scorch the food. Choice of frying pan is also important: thin pans must be kept moving, used with great delicacy.

When I fry, I carefully prepare my ingredients and equipment, and ensure that everything is ready and within reach. I then rake out a small bed of embers to the side of the fire and begin, never allowing my concentration to wander until the frying is complete.

Frying requires an interface between the hot pan and the food, usually oil or fat. The transfer of heat from the hot pan is very rapid, which means it's a cooking method best suited to thin ingredients; ones thicker than about 2.5cm (1in) may cook on the surface but remain uncooked in their core. In the home kitchen, this can be avoided by starting the frying over a hob and then transferring the pan to an oven to finish off, but of course that option is rarely available on the trail.

SUCCESSFUL FRYING

Frying outdoors in many ways requires a higher degree of skill than when cooking indoors, particularly when using a lightweight frying pan. So, following Marshal Zhukov's maxim 'Train hard, fight easy', we shall explore how to cook with a thin pan successfully. As always when cooking outdoors, we must search for advantages to help us achieve the desired result.

CHOICE OF OIL

The first of these is our choice of oil. What we need is an oil with a high smoke point – oils that remain stable at high temperatures (see chart below). Where possible, try to avoid cholesterol-raising saturated fats.

Groundnut oil, if we can carry it, provides a significant advantage when cooking outdoors, most especially when stir-frying. There will, however, be times when there is no choice. If the only oil available is extra virgin olive oil, it is still possible to fry, but considerable extra care will need to be taken to avoid the oil overheating, especially on a campfire.

The smoke points of oils

OIL	SMOKE POINT		OIL	SMOKE POINT	
Extra-light olive	240°C	464°F			
Groundnut	230°C	446°F	Rapeseed	205°C	401°F
Ghee*	230°C	446°F	Tallow	205°C	401°F
Vegetable	230°C	446°F	Olive	200°C	392°F
Corn	230°C	446°F	Lard*	185°C	365°F
Palm	230°C	446°F	Coconut	175°C	347°F
Sunflower	225°C	437°F	Butter*	175°C	347°F
Margarine	220°C	428°F	Extra virgin olive	160°C	320°F

* = saturated fats

FRYING BASICS

1 Heat the pan over a moderate heat.
2 Add the oil and heat until it shimmers.
3 Add the prepared food. If the oil is hot enough, it will sizzle upon contact.
4 Keep stirring and flipping the food (excepting whole fish and fish steaks).
5 Remove the pan from the heat at the first sign of smoking oil.
6 Keep moving the food, since it will still be frying.
7 Serve as soon as the frying is complete.

Top tip: always concentrate until the frying is done!

SIZE OF INGREDIENTS

Given that frying favours thin ingredients, try to cut them to an appropriate size to begin with. However, if this is not possible – for instance, if you have a thick fish steak – there is a way to tackle it and still produce succulent results (see page 107).

TURNING THE FOOD

Generally, it is best to keep the food moving in the pan. The exception is frying fish, in which case it is better to only turn the fish over once as it is more delicate.

AVOID AN OVERCROWDED PAN

If you load the pan with too many ingredients, moisture cannot escape and the food will steam rather than fry. This is particularly relevant when browning meat, which may best be achieved in small batches.

HOW TO FRY AN EGG

Eggs cook very quickly, making them an ideal food for the trail. The great mistake is to cook them over too high a heat. Instead, start them cooking in oil heated in a frying pan over a moderate heat, then immediately remove the pan from the heat, using its residual heat to complete the cooking. Even a thin pan usually has enough residual heat for this process to work. If not, the cooking will slow, at which point tickle the pan with some more heat as necessary. Done correctly, the eggs will not stick to the pan or scorch.

HOW TO STIR-FRY

A stir-fry is a wonderful thing, producing colourful, crunchy and delicious food in no time at all. In fact, most of the time involved with making one is taken up in the preparation of the ingredients, which need to be cut into small, easily cooked pieces. Stir-frying is also great for wilderness cooking because it's easy to produce the high heat that best suits this technique. Use an oil with a high smoke point – groundnut is perfect. While stir-frying, keep both the wok and the ingredients moving.

HOW TO FRY A STEAK

1 Begin by seasoning the steak with salt and ground black pepper – consider hunter's salt (see page 52). I also like to rub the surface of the steak with good balsamic vinegar.

2 Set aside while you prepare the fire and cook all of the other elements of the meal.

3 Heat the pan – a heavy pan is best, or the lid of a camp oven. If you are cooking several steaks, use the largest pan you have. If the steaks are overcrowded, they will steam and be disappointing. If you only have one small frying pan, cook the steaks one at a time.

4 Add the oil – groundnut is excellent for this – and heat until it shimmers.

5 Add the steak to the pan and follow the usual rules of not allowing the oil to smoke. Cook for 1 minute, then turn and cook for 1 minute more.

6 Keep turning until the steak is cooked to your liking (see page 258).

7 Remove the steak(s) from the pan and place in a warm place to rest for 5 minutes.

8 Meanwhile, deglaze the pan and make a gravy (see page 263).

HOW TO DRY-FRY A FISH FILLET

If you are short of oil, fish fillets can be cooked in a dry pan.

1 First, descale the fish skin. Heat the pan and then sprinkle salt across the surface – coarse salt is best if you have it.

2 Add the fillet to the pan skin side down and cook for 2–3 minutes, until the fillet is opaque two-thirds of the way through and the skin has a good colour.

3 Lift the fillet, refresh the salt and cook the flesh side until opaque and cooked through.

HOW TO FRY A THIN FISH FILLET

1 Prepare the fish by descaling the skin side of the fillet. Salt the fillet on both sides. This firms up the flesh, as well as seasoning it.

2 Prepare all the other ingredients.

3 Heat the frying pan over a moderate heat.

4 Dry off the fillet with kitchen paper, if you have it.

5 Heat the oil and when it shimmers, add the fillet skin side down to the pan. Cook until the flesh appears to have turned opaque two-thirds of the way through its thickness. You may need to press on the fillet occasionally to prevent it from curling upwards.

6 Now flip the fillet and carry on frying until the fish is opaque all the way through. At no stage allow the oil to smoke.

7 Do not turn the fillet again. Serve as soon as the fish is cooked through and flakes easily.

HOW TO FRY A THICK FISH STEAK

1 A thick steak of salmon, for example, requires a slightly different approach. Prepare the fish and any other ingredients.

2 Put a little water in a dry frying pan, then place it over a moderate heat. Place the steak in the pan and simmer until the water has evaporated.

3 At this point, add a generous knob of butter to the pan and fry the steak until it has good colour, turning it just once.

4 While the steak is frying, season it with angler's salt (see page 52) and some ground black pepper.

5 Serve the fish steak as soon as it is cooked through and opaque. Boiled potatoes and peas garnished with lemon wedges and wild chickweed make excellent accompaniments.

CANOE CAMP FISHCAKES

This recipe reflects the spartan nature of catering on a canoe trip, but do not be of faint heart for these fishcakes are a firm favourite, being both filling and delicious. I usually wait for a day when the weather has been bad or the portages long to serve this meal. The only problem is that you will be asked for more, and then there is the dilemma of whether or not to make more now or look forward to eating them again further down the paddle? I guess there are worse problems to have.

INGREDIENTS

Makes 8–10 fishcakes

1 cup (100g) dehydrated
   powdered mashed
   potato
213g (7½oz) can wild
   Alaskan salmon
1 tsp dried mixed herbs
good pinch of angler's
   salt (see page 52)
good pinch of ground
   black pepper
flour, for rolling
groundnut oil, high
   temp olive oil or
   vegetable oil, for
   frying

METHOD

1 Reconstitute the dehydrated potato following the packet instructions.
2 Add the salmon, herbs and seasoning and mix it all together with your hands.
3 Roll into small balls, 5cm (2in) in diameter.
4 Roll each ball in some flour and then flatten into a fishcake.
5 Heat the pan, then the oil, and fry the fishcakes for about 3 minutes on each side, until golden and crispy.

VARIATIONS

■ If your fishing has been successful, use well-filleted and carefully deboned fresh fish instead of the canned salmon, and add 1 tbsp of reconstituted egg powder to help bind it all together.

■ If you have the foraging skill, look for some fresh herbs to incorporate. Even a pinch of very finely chopped spruce needles will work.

TIPSY TROUT

This is a simple recipe that's easy and quick to cook, even on a stove at the water's edge. Despite the speed and simplicity, however, it really honours the fish.

INGREDIENTS

Serves 2

2 skin-on trout fillets (or any salmonid can be used)
angler's salt (see page 52)
3 tbsp butter
brandy (I'll leave the quantity up to you. The fish should be merry, not drunk!)
1½ cups (375ml) cream or crème fraîche
boiled potatoes or rice and peas, to serve
wild bitter cress, to garnish (optional)

METHOD

1 Season the fillets all over with angler's salt.
2 Heat a frying pan over a moderate heat, then add the butter and heat until just foaming.
3 Add the fish and fry on each side just until the skin is golden.
4 Add the brandy to the pan and ignite by tipping the pan slightly so the brandy just catches in the flame. Take care!
5 When the flames are out, stir in the cream or crème fraîche and simmer until the fish is cooked. Check by piercing with the tip of a knife. The flesh should be opaque and flake easily.
6 Serve with boiled potatoes or rice and peas. Garnish with wild bitter cress, if you have some.

CHICKEN SUPRÊME

Classically, the suprême is served as a whole breast with the sauce ladled over, with the first wing bone still attached, in which case it is a chicken côtelette. Outdoors, where we lack a fine dining room, however, it is more convenient to slice the rested chicken breast before adding the sauce. This dish is wonderful when accompanied by rice or potatoes and some foraged greens. My preference is to cook the côtelette with the skin on, as shown.

INGREDIENTS

Serves 4

2 shallots
2 garlic cloves
handful of
    mushrooms
4 chicken breasts
flour, for dusting
oil, for frying
1 cup (250ml) chicken
    stock (see page 261),
    or ½ cup (125ml)
    each of stock
    and white wine,
    if possible
1 cup (250ml) cream
2 tsp good balsamic
    vinegar
4 tbsp chopped
    parsley
salt and ground black
    pepper, to taste
rice or potatoes
    and some foraged
    greens, to serve

METHOD

1 Peel and chop the shallots and garlic. Wipe clean and slice or quarter the mushrooms, depending on size and type.
2 Season the chicken breasts all over, then liberally dust with flour.
3 Heat the oil in a frying pan over a gentle heat, then add the chicken breasts and fry until golden all over. If the pan is small, rather than overcrowding the pan, cook the breasts in batches.
4 Set the cooked chicken breasts aside in a warm pan.
5 In the remaining oil in the frying pan, fry the shallots, garlic and mushrooms for about 8 minutes, until softened and light golden. Put a lid on the pan to sweat the mushrooms for their flavour.
6 Add the balsamic vinegar.
7 Deglaze the pan with a cup of stock, or better still, white wine if it is available. Add the remaining stock.

8 Return the chicken breasts to the pan and simmer for 10 minutes, or until cooked through.
9 Remove the chicken to the warm pan and allow to rest.
10 Add the cream to give the sauce body, then season the sauce to taste and stir in the chopped parsley.
11 Serve the chicken breast whole, or sliced for convenience, with the sauce ladled over it and some cooked rice or potatoes and foraged greens.

JÄGERSCHNITZEL

The Hunter's Cutlet was originally made from venison back steak sliced thin and gently pounded flat and to even thickness. Here I am using pork for convenience. Serve this lovely dish with a green salad and mashed potato or in the simple true hunter's style with rustic crusty bread.

INGREDIENTS

Serves 4

1 onion
handful of
  mushrooms
4 pork loin steaks
5 tbsp olive oil
2 tbsp flour
1 cup (250ml) red
  wine (optional),
  or use the same
  quantity of extra
  beef stock
1 cup (250ml) beef
  stock (see page 262)
3 tbsp sour cream
handful of chopped
  parsley
salt and ground black
  pepper, to taste
finely chopped edible
  greens, to garnish
  (optional)

METHOD

1 Peel and slice the onion, then wipe clean and slice or quarter the mushrooms, depending on size and type.
2 Gently pound the pork loin to tenderise the meat and achieve an even 5mm (¼in) thickness across the steaks. Season on both sides.
3 In a frying pan, heat 2 tbsp of the oil, then add the flour and create a blonde roux. Cook for 2 minutes, stirring, then remove this from the pan and allow to cool.
4 In the frying pan, heat 2 tbsp of the oil, then add the onion and cook over a low heat for about 15 minutes, until translucent and soft.
5 Add the mushrooms and continue cooking for another 10 minutes or so, until nicely coloured.
6 Meanwhile, prepare the stock. Set aside 1 cup (250ml) if you don't have wine available for later use. Put the remainder in a pan over a medium heat and once hot, gradually add the cooled roux in small pieces, whisking well so it dissolves and to avoid lumps.
7 Add the red wine or reserved

stock to the onions and mushrooms and deglaze the pan.
8 Transfer everything from the frying pan into the thickened stock and stir to combine, then continue cooking to reduce the gravy to the desired consistency.
9 While the gravy is reducing, add 1 tbsp of the oil to the frying pan and fry the meat over a medium heat for about 5 minutes on each side, or until brown all over and cooked through.
10 Stir the sour cream and chopped parsley into the gravy to finish. Serve the cutlets with the gravy poured over and garnish with edible greens, if you like.

MEATBALLS

Meatballs take some preparation but cook very quickly and are wonderful served with mashed potato or plain rice. When I finish cooking the meatballs, I deglaze the pan with a splash of alcohol (cognac by choice), and then add a touch of cream and stock to make a wonderful gravy.

INGREDIENTS

Serves 4

3 cups (750ml) evaporated milk

2 cups (250g) fresh breadcrumbs

1 medium onion

4 tbsp butter

500g (1lb) minced beef or venison

1 egg, lightly beaten

large pinch of hunter's salt (see page 52)

large pinch of ground black pepper

1 tbsp balsamic vinegar (optional)

mashed potatoes, Gravy From Scratch (see page 263) and redcurrant jelly (optional), to serve

METHOD

1 Mix the evaporated milk with the breadcrumbs and set aside to soak for about 10 minutes. If necessary, add a little water – the breadcrumbs should be soaked through.

2 Meanwhile, peel and finely chop the onion.

3 Put 1 tbsp of the butter in a frying pan and heat until melted. Add the onion and cook for about 15 minutes until translucent and soft. Remove to a bowl and leave to cool.

4 Add the meat to the onions along with the egg, breadcrumb mixture, hunter's salt and black pepper. I sometimes add a little balsamic vinegar, too.

5 Combine everything well with your hands, then fashion into meatballs measuring about 3cm (1½in) in diameter.

6 Heat the remaining butter in the frying pan until foaming, then add the meatballs and fry over a medium heat until cooked through and golden brown.

7 Serve with mashed potatoes, gravy and redcurrant jelly, if you have any.

SPAGHETTI CARBONARA

True carbonara is made in this way without the need for any cream. Take care not to overcook the sauce or it will turn to scrambled eggs – make sure the pan is off the heat and serve the spaghetti immediately.

INGREDIENTS

Serves 2

about 150g (5oz) dried spaghetti (depending on appetite)
few rashers of pancetta or bacon
1 tbsp olive oil
2 eggs
4–6 tbsp grated pecorino cheese
Parmesan cheese and ground black pepper, to serve

METHOD

1 Bring a pan of lightly salted water to the boil, then add the spaghetti and cook for about 8 minutes or according to the packet instructions, until al dente.

2 Meanwhile, dice the pancetta or bacon into 1cm (½in) cubes. In a wide pan or frying pan, heat the oil and fry the pancetta or bacon over a medium heat until golden.

3 Meanwhile, in a separate pan or bowl, prepare the sauce by whisking the eggs and adding the pecorino.

4 Once the pancetta or bacon has a nice colour, take it off the heat.

5 Drain the spaghetti, then add it to the pan of pancetta or bacon and mix to combine.

6 Add the sauce and then fold it into the pasta. The spaghetti should have cooled a little but should retain enough heat to cook the sauce through.

7 Grate some Parmesan over the finished dish and grind over some black pepper to serve.

SCRAMBLED EGGS

Cooked properly, the pan will be clean and the scrambled eggs beautifully creamy. This is a quick, satisfying meal that makes great cabin fare when you are hungry but in a hurry or very tired. It's lovely served with hot buttered toast.

INGREDIENTS

Serves 2

4 eggs
⅖ cup (100ml) milk
2 tbsp butter
salt and ground black pepper, to taste

METHOD

1 Lightly beat the eggs in a bowl, then add the milk and salt and ground black pepper to taste.

2 Melt the butter in the pan over a gentle heat, then pour in the beaten eggs.

3 Keep the mixture moving with a spatula, then when the eggs begin to scramble, remove the pan from the heat. Use the residual heat in the pan to complete the cooking. If the cooking slows, give the pan a tickle over your heat source.

OMELETTE IN A SCRUFFY PAN

More often than not, our pan has seen hard service and is unwilling to work subtle miracles of French gastronomy, so here is a country recipe to irritate the perfectionists but delight your fellow diners. Most importantly, it will work in most pans within sensible reason!

INGREDIENTS

Serves 1

flavour ingredient, such as cheese and/or ham and/or mushrooms
1 tbsp butter, plus extra for frying
2–3 eggs (depending on the size of the pan)
pinch each of salt and ground black pepper

METHOD

1 Finely grate the cheese and/or dice the ham and/or wipe, slice and sauté the mushrooms in a little butter.
2 Whisk the eggs until well aerated, then add a pinch each of salt and ground black pepper and the main ingredient and fold into the eggs.
3 Heat the pan over a medium heat, then add 1 tbsp butter. Once foaming, pour in the egg mix and cook gently, moving the mixture with the back of a fork.

4 As soon as the omelette starts to come together, remove from the heat and rely on the pan's residual heat to finish off. If the cooking slows, tickle the pan with your heat source. Do not overcook the omelette: remember, it's a light dish.
5 Fold the omelette and slide it onto a plate.

below Autumn is a wonderful time for the wilderness chef because of the abundance of edible wild mushrooms.

OMELETTE IN A PRISTINE PAN

The classic way to make an omelette, it requires skill, delicacy and concentration to make it right. It also needs a pan in perfect condition – clean, smooth and well seasoned. It has been said many times that when you can do this you can cook anything. It is even more difficult outdoors. Good luck!

INGREDIENTS

Serves 1

flavour ingredient, such as cheese and/or ham and/or mushrooms
butter for frying, if using mushrooms
2–3 eggs (depending on the size of the pan)
1 tbsp water
1 tbsp butter
salt and ground black pepper, to taste

METHOD

1 Prepare your main ingredient(s). If cheese, finely grate it. If ham, dice it. If mushrooms, wipe clean, slice and sauté in a little butter with seasoning until coloured.
2 Lightly beat the eggs, then season to taste, add the water and then mix to combine.
3 Heat the pan, add the butter and heat until foaming.
4 Pour in the egg mix. As soon as the eggs begin to coagulate, agitate the pan first with a circular motion, then add the flavouring ingredient(s) to the centre of the omelette. Finish with a more linear backwards-and-forwards motion, which will fold the omelette. The trick is to keep it moving until it's cooked, it only takes seconds.
5 Slide the omelette onto a plate. It should be light and still soft in the middle.

Cook's tip
Too much egg in one go leads to a slowly cooked omelette, which will be rubbery. When cooking many omelettes, therefore, spoon the egg into the pan with a ladle to get the quantity just right, rather than dolloping in haphazardly.

VARIATIONS

■ Omelettes are an incredibly versatile meal and can be filled with many wonderful ingredients, such as shellfish, bacon bits or chopped fresh herbs. If any ingredients need to be cooked, such as shellfish or bacon, they must be cooked before they are incorporated into the eggs.

■ Edible wild plants and mushrooms work well. My favourites are fat hen omelette and bacon and nettle omelette. For the latter, use the freshest nettle tops gathered from a shady location (these will be less bitter). Blanch them in boiling water for 60 seconds. Drain them well and chop finely before using.

TORTILLA ESPAÑOLA
OR SPANISH OMELETTE

The quantities given here are for my favourite trail pan, which is small – only 22cm (9in) in diameter. You will have to scale up for a larger pan, but this is one of those recipes that is made by intuitive judgement rather than micro measurement. It is wonderful as part of a lunch in a fixed camp, served with salad, pickled ingredients and cold meats. No doubt you will improvise with what you have. If all that is available to you is tinned meat, this tortilla will elevate the whole meal. The tortilla itself can be made with reconstituted egg powder if push comes to shove, but it is a poor second to real eggs.

INGREDIENTS

Serves 2

1 potato
1 onion (optional)
4 tbsp olive oil
2–3 eggs (depending on the size of your pan)
salt and ground black pepper, to taste

METHOD

1 Peel and finely chop the potato and onion. While the onion lends flavour, it is not essential to the omelette.

2 Heat 2 tbsp of the oil in a wide billycan or frying pan over a medium heat, then add the potato and onion, if using. Shallow-fry for about 15 minutes, until soft. (I use a billycan as the frying pan I carry is not deep enough to shallow-fry the ingredients safely.)

3 While the potato and onion are cooking, beat the eggs and add the seasoning to the bowl.

4 Once cooked through, drain the potato and onion with a slotted spoon and add to the egg mixture. Fold them in well.

5 Heat your frying pan or billycan lid over a low heat, add the remaining oil and, once hot, pour in the egg mixture.

6 Cook gently. The aim is to cook the tortilla two-thirds through without scorching the base. Beware the ultra-thin pan!

7 Once the tortilla becomes sufficiently solid to turn over, place a plate over the pan, then invert both together. All being well, the tortilla will be sitting on the plate and can be slid back into the pan to complete cooking.

8 When finished, place a clean plate on top of the pan and flip it over to turn out the finished tortilla.

VARIATION

Alternatively, the potato can be grated and fried in less oil in a frying pan. This is a method that suits cooking on a hike stove as less fuel will be consumed.

EGGS BENEDICT

This recipe should need no introduction. Outdoors it requires some effort to cook but is a wonderful recipe to lift the mood, celebrate a birthday or some other special occasion. Should your hollandaise split, whisk in a spoonful of boiling water.

INGREDIENTS

Serves 1

1 toasting muffin
a little olive oil, if
   using bacon
2 slices of bacon or
   ham – serrano or
   canned Canadian, all
   types are acceptable
2 poached eggs (see
   page 160)
hollandaise sauce (see
   page 264)
ground black pepper

METHOD

1 Slice the muffin in half, then toast over the fire on a stick or brown in a lightly oiled frying pan. Remove to a plate.
2 Heat the oil and fry the bacon or ham in the frying pan.
3 Top the muffins first with bacon or ham and then the poached eggs.
4 Liberally top with hollandaise sauce. Finish with a sprinkle of ground black pepper.

VARIATIONS

IRISH BENEDICT Replace the ham with corned beef slices.

EGGS ROYALE Replace the ham with sliced smoked salmon.

BUSHCRAFT BENEDICT Replace the ham with blanched stinging nettle tops.

ROSTI POTATO

This is an easy dish to cook outdoors. Be gentle with the heat and take your time. It is delicious served with salad and meat from the griddle.

INGREDIENTS

Serves 4

2 large potatoes
1 onion (optional)
1 egg yolk (optional)
4 tbsp olive oil or
   butter
salt and ground black
   pepper, to taste

METHOD

1 Peel the potatoes and onion, then coarsely grate the potato and finely chop the onion. Squeeze all of it to remove as much liquid as possible. Place in a bowl and stir to combine.

2 Stir in the egg yolk, if using. This will help to bind the ingredients. It is also possible to use reconstituted egg powder here or simply to cook the rosti without the egg at all.

3 Heat the frying pan over a medium heat, then add half the oil or butter and heat until sizzling.

4 Add the potato and onion mix, then compress the mixture using the back of a large spoon to form a flat disc.

5 Cook gently over a low heat, without scorching, for about 15 minutes or until the rosti is strong enough to turn over and is golden on the underside.

6 Place a plate on top of the pan, then flip it and the pan. The rosti should turn out onto the plate. Add the remaining oil or butter to the pan and slide the rosti back into the pan to cook on the other side.

7 When golden – about 10 minutes – turn out onto a clean plate or cutting board. Leave to cool slightly, then slice and serve.

STIR-FRIED VEGETABLES

A wok is a cumbersome cooking pan to carry, so it's best suited to the fixed or base camp set-up. Nevertheless, it's well worth having along. Stir-frying is a wonderful way to cook all manner of foods: it is incredibly versatile, healthy and delicious. What's more, many wild ingredients respond well to this method of cooking. If you like Asian-style food it is worth familiarising yourself with Asian ingredients such as oyster sauce, fish sauce and rice wine vinegar. This recipe only calls for soy and hoisin sauces in addition to our other basic fixed-camp ingredients. Add some chillies, cashew nuts and chicken or tofu to this recipe and you have a basic kung po with mixed vegetables. Serve immediately with cooked rice or noodles.

INGREDIENTS

broccoli florets
carrots, peeled and cut
   into matchsticks
red pepper, seeded
   and cut into thin
   strips
yellow pepper, seeded
   and cut into thin
   strips
onion, peeled and
   cut into crescents
2–3 garlic cloves,
   peeled and finely
   chopped
small knob of fresh
   root ginger, peeled
   and finely chopped
star anise (optional)
red chilli, seeded
   and finely chopped
   (optional)
groundnut oil, for
   stir-frying
cooked rice or
   noodles, to serve

For the sauce
1 tbsp balsamic
   vinegar
1 tsp dark soy
   sauce
1 tsp hoisin sauce
1 tsp sesame oil
2 tsp sugar or
   honey
2 tbsp cornflour
2 tbsp water

METHOD

1 Prepare all of the vegetables. The secret to stir-frying is to have all the ingredients cut to a uniform size so that they cook evenly. Combine all the sauce ingredients in a bowl.

2 Blanch the vegetables (not the garlic, ginger or chilli) in a large billycan of boiling water to the point where they are just reaching tenderness. This will preserve their colour and ensure that they are properly cooked. It's especially useful if you are cooking for lots of people and the wok is quite full when you come to stir-fry the veg.

3 Drain all of the vegetables well.

4 Heat the wok, add the oil and heat, ensuring that all of the wok surface has been coated in oil.

5 Over a moderate heat, add the garlic and ginger and cook to release their aromas. Keep them moving so that they do not burn. At this stage, you might also add a star anise.

6 Add the sauce and cook until the garlic is soft.

7 Now add the vegetables, starting with the hardest and slowest-cooking (broccoli and carrots) and working your way through to the softest. Finish with the chilli.

8 Using high heat, keep the wok and the ingredients moving. Cook until golden and tender.

9 Serve immediately with rice or noodles.

LEBANESE BREAD

Lebanese flatbread isn't only fun to cook outdoors, but is also a versatile bread and an ideal accompaniment to a curry or fish cooked over a fire.

INGREDIENTS

Makes 4–6

1 tsp fast-action dried yeast
½ cup (125ml) warm water
1 tsp sugar
1–2 cups (125–250g) strong white bread flour, plus extra for dusting
1 tbsp olive oil, plus extra for greasing
¾ tsp salt

METHOD

1 In a mixing bowl, combine the yeast and the water, then stir in the sugar and ½ cup (60g) of the flour. Cover and leave until bubbles form in the mixture.

2 Add the olive oil, salt and the remaining flour a little at a time until a nice dough is formed, which lifts easily from the bowl and is only very slightly sticky. The amount of flour you need will vary according to type, so assess it as you add it.

3 Turn the dough onto a floured surface and knead it for 5–10 minutes until smooth and elastic.

4 Oil or flour the mixing bowl, place the dough in it and cover. Leave to prove in a warm (not hot) place until doubled in size – about 2 hours, but it depends on conditions.

5 Turn out the dough onto a floured surface and cut it into segments that can be rolled into 5cm- (2in)-diameter balls.

6 Set a frying pan on a fire to heat. Alternatively, if you have a wok, invert it over a stove or small fire.

7 Roll out the balls on the floured surface into 20cm- (8in)-diameter circles. With floured hands, flip these backwards and forwards over your wrists to make the rounds larger and very thin. (Traditionally, these are spread over a special pillow and spread even thinner, the pillow then being used to transfer the dough to the pan. We shall leave out this stage.)

8 The round can now be dropped into a very hot frying pan or on the base of the very hot wok and cooked for 30–60 seconds until puffed up and cooked through. Serve warm.

PLAIN BANNOCK

This is essentially the same recipe as for Damper (see pages 58–9) or Campfire Bread (see pages 74–5), but this time it is cooked in a frying pan beside the fire or on a prop stick beside a wood-burning stove.

INGREDIENTS

Makes 1

2 cups (250g) plain or
self-raising flour
2 tsp baking powder
1 tsp salt
2 tbsp butter or
vegetable oil, plus
extra for greasing
about ⅔ cup (175ml)
cold water

METHOD

1 In a bowl, combine the dry ingredients well, then rub in the butter or oil using your fingertips.
2 Add enough cold water to form a dry dough.
3 Lightly oil a frying pan and heat it over the fire.
4 Form the dough into a ball and then flatten it out in the pan until it is thumb thick.
5 Begin the cooking over a medium-low heat. I rake out some embers at the edge of the fire for this.
6 Once the bannock begins cooking it will start to solidify and can be shaken loose from the pan base, making it easy to flip it later. At this point, tilt the pan and prop it towards the heat at the edge of the fire.
7 Flip and rotate the bannock as necessary until it is cooked through. Test using a skewer: when it can be drawn out dry, the bannock is ready.

VARIATIONS

■ Although it's great to include butter, oil or lard in a winter bannock recipe, it can equally be made without, if it is not available.
■ Dried meat, cheese or herbs can all be added to the recipe as the fancy takes you.

SWEET BANNOCK

This sweet version is a perennial favourite in camp. The method of cooking is identical to that of a plain bannock. Fold the dried fruit into the dough once it has been formed.

INGREDIENTS:
2 cups (250g) plain or self-raising flour
1 cup (125g) milk powder
2 tsp baking powder
2 tsp sugar
about ⅔ cup (175ml) cold water
½ cup (75g) dried fruit

PITA BREAD

Homemade pita pockets filled with strips of crispy fried bacon, rocket, tomato, mayonnaise and black pepper make a world-class dish. They taste pretty good on their own, or perhaps simply drizzled with some oil, too.

INGREDIENTS

Makes 6–8

1 cup (250ml) water
1 tsp fast-action dried yeast
about 3 cups (375g) strong white bread flour, plus extra for dusting
1½ tbsp olive oil, plus extra for greasing
1½ tsp salt

METHOD

1 Place the water in a mixing bowl, add the yeast and whisk together well. Mix in 1 cup (125g) of the flour.

2 Cover the bowl and leave to rest for a few minutes to allow the yeast to activate. You should see bubbles in the mixture.

3 Add the olive oil and the salt, then little by little add more flour, mixing all the time, until you have a nice dough that is only slightly sticky and will lift away from the mixing bowl easily.

4 Turn out the dough onto a floured surface and knead it for 5–10 minutes, until smooth and elastic.

5 Grease the bowl, return the dough to it, cover and leave to prove in a warm (not hot) place until doubled in size – about 2 hours, longer in cold weather.

6 Turn out the dough onto a floured surface, then flatten it and break off pieces to form small oval buns measuring about 6 x 10cm (2½–4in). Form these by tucking the edges under.

7 Cover and leave to rest for 30 minutes, then roll out the dough to 5mm (¼in) thickness. Leave to rest for another 5 minutes.

8 Meanwhile, heat a frying pan over a fire and grease well with oil.

9 Cook the breads one at a time in the hot frying pan. Give them approximately 3 minutes on each side. Turn again and allow them to puff up. Set aside and repeat until all of the dough is cooked.

WELSH CAKES

These traditional cakes from the mountains and valleys of beautiful Wales are wonderful on a wilderness journey. A batch made in the evening is always well received on a canoe trip, particularly when you have been paddling into a headwind all morning.

INGREDIENTS

Makes 4–6

1 cup (125g) self-raising flour
pinch of salt
¼ cup (50g) sugar
½ tsp mixed spice (optional)
6 tbsp butter or margarine, plus extra for greasing
2 tbsp milk powder
2 tbsp powdered egg
4 tbsp water
4 tbsp currants

METHOD

1 Aerate the flour by whisking it in a bowl with a fork, then whisk in the salt, sugar and the mixed spice, if using.

2 Dice the butter or margarine and then work it into the mixture with your fingertips.

3 Whisk the milk powder and powdered egg into the water and when well mixed, stir into the cake mix.

4 Add the currants and work into the mixture.

5 With your hands, roll the mixture into balls slightly larger than a walnut and flatten into round cakes.

6 Grease a camp oven lid or frying pan with a little butter or margarine. Cook the cakes over a gentle heat until golden brown on both sides. These also cook well in a reflector oven.

CORN PONE

Corn Pone or Indian Corn Bread is a more refined version of Johnny Cake (see page 87) – the same basic recipe elevated with the benefit of more ingredients. This can also be made as a thick dough and cooked on a board, but is usually fried. It is a traditional accompaniment to meat dishes in Native American cuisine.

INGREDIENTS

Serves 4

1 cup (150g) cornmeal
½ tsp salt
1 tbsp butter or lard
1 cup (250ml) boiling
  water
2 tbsp oil

METHOD

1 In a bowl, mix the cornmeal and the salt, then add the butter or lard and rub it into the dry mixture.
2 Stir in the boiling water and leave to absorb for 10 minutes. If necessary, add more water to relax the mixture. You are aiming for a batter that's twice as thick as pancake batter.
3 Heat the oil in a frying pan over a moderate heat. Spoon the batter into the pan to form biscuit-sized cakes about 1cm (½in) thick.
4 Cook for a few minutes until the cakes can be turned. Now, cook on the other side until golden and cooked through. Serve hot.

VARIATION

You can improve the recipe by adding 1 tbsp milk powder and 1 tsp baking powder for a little lift.

CHAPATI

These flat breads are really simple to make and cook, and are multifunctional. Brush with some melted butter to accompany spicy dishes, or split them and use like pita pockets.

INGREDIENTS

Makes 8–10 chapati

2 cups (280g) plain flour, plus extra for dusting
1 tsp salt
1 tbsp vegetable oil
1 cups (250ml) water

METHOD

1 In a bowl, mix the dry ingredients well, then add the oil and stir in.
2 Now, little by little, add the water until you have a smooth dough. Only use sufficient water to achieve the dough.
3 Knead the dough very gently for 2–3 minutes to bring it into a ball, then cover and leave to rest for 10 minutes.
4 Turn the dough out onto a floured surface and knead well for 5 minutes, until smooth and elastic.
5 Break off sections of dough and roll between your palms to form balls about the size of a lime, 5cm (2in) in diameter.
6 On a floured surface, roll these out one at a time to a 15cm (6in) circle. Pat off any excess flour.

7 Cook on a heated frying pan or griddle over a low heat until bubbles form in the chapati, 45–60 seconds. Turn and cook for the same amount of time on the other side.
8 Remove to a plate and repeat the process to cook all of the breads.

VARIATION

If cooking over a jet burner, place the bread directly over the burner. The chapati will inflate. If cooking over a fire, increase the heat to the pan for the same result.

CANOE COUNTRY PANCAKES

British chefs will recognise this as a larger version of the traditional drop scone. The size reflects the calorific demands of paddling all day. This quick-and-easy recipe is a great way to start the day, but just because it is easy, do not forget that it requires good organisation. I once participated in a trip that was to be catered for by a young professional guide. On the first day out, he delayed our party struggling with his fire in the rain before eventually serving pancakes cooked like rubber on the outside, uncooked on the inside and swimming in a plate of rainwater. Not his best day, and a poor way to establish the confidence of the party, which was comprised of some of the most experienced canoeists in the world. I am glad to say that he earned our respect later on by swallowing his pride and asking for tuition. We were all young once!

INGREDIENTS

Serves 2–4

2 cups (250g) self-
  raising flour
4 tbsp milk powder
2 tsp baking powder
4 tbsp powdered egg
pinch of salt
4 tbsp sugar
about 1 cup (250ml)
  water
2 tbsp butter or oil
handful of dried fruit
  or fresh berries
maple syrup or runny
  honey, to serve

METHOD

1 Aerate the flour by whisking it in a bowl with a fork, then add the milk powder, baking powder, powdered egg, salt and sugar.
2 Add the water and mix to produce a batter with the consistency of double cream.
3 Heat a frying pan or griddle over a medium heat, then add a little butter or oil and ladle out a pancake 15cm (6in) in diameter.
4 Sprinkle fruit on the surface of the pancake.

5 Cook gently until bubbles begin to break evenly from the surface of the pancake, then use a spatula to turn the pancake. Cook for a similar amount of time on the reverse side.
6 Serve drizzled with maple syrup or runny honey.

BOILING

IT IS STRANGE TO THINK but for the vast majority of human history we lived without access to a cooking pot. Even in more recent history, there remained communities where boiling was only achievable by taking rocks heated in a fire, and placing them into water contained in a bark, wood or skin vessel. When travelling, fragile birch bark cooking containers had to be carefully handled, particularly in winter, when they could not be easily replaced.

There are accounts of Native Canadian women digging into snowdrifts in search of pot boiling rocks left behind in the summer. In Australia, some Aboriginal communities did not boil food at all until the arrival of modern cooking pots, while in Hokkaido there are accounts of people cooking tea in a folded butterbur leaf. The fact that humanity managed for so long without a cooking pot is a testimony to the hardiness, skill and ingenuity of our forebears. Studying the skills of our ancestors has made me acutely appreciative of the tools of today.

Today we take a simple billy can for granted, yet it is arguably the single most important outdoor cooking utensil. With a cooking pot in the remote wilderness we are wealthy, able to boil water at will to make it safe to drink. With hot water we can improve the flavour and edibility of wild foods, we can create beverages, make stocks, soups and sauces and of course cook staple foods with ease.

Boiling has the advantage of preserving many of the ingredients' nutrients while reducing the risk of scorching or burning the food. But do not think that it is as simple as throwing ingredients into boiling water; there is skill in boiling, as always there are things to know. Do it wrong and the food will be flavourless or chewy, like an old rubber tyre. While done right, food will be tender and moist, packed with a kaleidoscope of intense flavours.

DRINKS

'The coffee alone is a common brew, always made in a kettle of copper with a lid on the spout, and always drunk sweetened with cone beet-sugar after the rest of the meal is finished. And when it is strong enough, Laplander's coffee is the best flavoured in Europe.'

ACROSS ARCTIC LAPLAND,
C. J. CUTCLIFFE HYNE, 1898

TEA

Tea: was there ever a more universal and life-sustaining beverage? The British Empire of old was built upon the stuff. In an age before antibiotics, the very process of boiling the water saved lives without measure, while the ritual of welcoming a stranger with a cup of tea was the essential ice-breaker of diplomacy, understood from the palaces of kings and maharajas to the windswept campfires of desert and mountain nomads. I have always felt that drinking tea outdoors connects me to a time when travel was riskier and more daring. Even today in the remote regions of the Commonwealth, this ancient rite still persists. I have many times been welcomed to a tea-filled kettle by the northern tribes inhabiting Canada's northern forest as equally as to the steaming billy in an Australian stock camp. When you are frozen to the core or parched and sun weary, tea is the finest welcome in the world and has a unique ability to connect people from different cultures.

As with so many simple rituals of the trail, there can be many hidden nuances in tea and how it is brewed. I well remember an old Australian stockman telling me how he had learned to make billy tea on his first day mending stock fencing out beyond the black stump. Given the job of brewing the crew's tea, he set to in the shade of a gum tree, only to be severely chided for not having made the fire out of the shade, where the sun was at its hottest and the tea would brew faster. 'Time is money, lad!'

Although when we talk of tea making we mostly refer to the use of dried leaves from the tea plant, *Camellia sinensis*, it is really the process that is important, that of infusing or decocting edible aromatic leaves. Consider, if you will, that almost anywhere we can kindle a fire we may be able to find a plant that can be used to make a wild herbal tea. For this reason alone, tea gets my vote as the number one outdoor beverage.

Today, we mostly carry teabags with us on the trail, since they are convenient to carry and apportion and remove any need for a strainer. A couple of Earl Grey teabags can be added to a kettle of boiled water and kept warm high over the fire for anyone to refresh with when returning to the camp. However, it is not so long ago that tea was carried loose and brewed using a mesh infuser, which is, conveniently, also perfect for brewing herbal teas made on the trail. Alternatively, loose tea can be used as described for Australian Billy Tea (see page 145).

The original packaging for tea to be transported into the wild was the tightly compressed tea brick. The first time I encountered this type was in Mongolia, where I watched with fascination a lady pulverising brick tea with a hammer. These tea bricks come in a variety of forms, the most robust being those made from powdered tea. Such bricks

are compact and highly resilient to the hazards of wilderness travel. They have an incredibly long shelf life and were once even traded as a form of currency. When needed, a sufficient quantity is simply grated from the edge of the brick with a knife. Allow 1 tsp per person plus 1 tsp for the pot. This powdered tea can be used immediately, although traditionally, it was given a momentary roasting in a pan to liberate its aromas. This traditional method may also have helped to destroy any mould or bacteria in the tea. It's easy to use: boil the kettle, remove from the heat and add the tea to infuse. After a few minutes, the tea can be poured. Alternatively, the tea can be brewed in milk.

Wild teas

Many wild plants can be used to make delicious herbal teas. While some teas can be brewed from fresh green parts, generally the best results are achieved by drying, which intensifies the flavour and makes it possible to store the tea for long periods in moisture-proof packaging.

At home, the best way to dry wild teas is with a dehydrator. In the field, they can be dried by being suspended in bundles in a warm, dry place or in a wide billycan set very high over the fire, in which case great care has to be exercised to prevent scorching. The table includes some of the best. With experience, you may decide to experiment with blends of different wild teas.

Wild teas and how to use them

COMMON NAME	SCIENTIFIC NAME	PARTS USED
bilberry	*Vaccinium myrtillus*	leaf • fruit
birch	*Betula spp.*	leaf • young twig
blackcurrant	*Ribes nigrum*	leaf • fruit
bramble	*Rubus fruticosus*	leaf
chaga	*Inonotus obliquus*	fruitbody
chamomile	*Chamaemelum nobile*	flower
clover	*Trifolium spp.*	flower
cowberry	*Vaccinium vitis-idaea*	leaf • fruit
elder	*Sambucus nigra*	flower
gorse	*Ulex europaeus*	flower
heather	*Calluna vulgaris*	flower
juniper	*Juniperus communis*	fruit
lime tree	*Tilia spp.*	leaf • flower
meadowsweet	*Filipendula ulmaria*	flower
mint	*Mentha spp.*	leaf
pine	*Pinus sylvestris*	needle
pineapple weed	*Matricaria discoidea*	flower
redcurrant	*Ribes rubrum*	leaf • fruit
spruce	*Picea abies*	needle • buds
stinging nettle	*Urtica dioica*	leaf
thyme	*Thymus spp.*	leaf
wild apple	*Malus sylvestris*	fruit
wild pear	*Pyrus pyraster*	fruit
wild raspberry	*Rubus idaeus*	leaf • stem
wild rose	*Rosa canina*	leaf • flower
wild strawberry	*Fragaria vesca*	leaf
willowherb	*Epilobium angustifolium*	leaf

AUSTRALIAN BILLY TEA

This is the classic way of making tea in the Outback: quick, easy and practical. The gum leaves lift the flavour, giving a quintessential Aussie twist. But if you don't have any? No worries, she'll be right without. Just make sure that the bail arm is strong enough for the spinning; the last thing you want to do is shower everyone with scalding tea.

INGREDIENTS

1 cup (250ml) water per person, plus 1 cup (250ml) for the pot
1 tbsp loose-leaf black tea per person, plus 1 tbsp for the pot
2 eucalyptus (gum) leaves
milk and sugar, to serve

METHOD

1 Bring the water to a rolling boil in the billycan for a minute. Remove the billycan from the fire and throw in the tea and the gum leaves. Allow the brew to steep for 2–3 minutes.
2 Take hold of the billy bail handle and swing the billycan around at arm's length, two or three full circles, to centrifuge the tea leaves to the billy's bottom. Allow to settle for a moment, then serve.
3 Each person can then add milk and sugar to their own taste.

LEMON TEA

When you are travelling in places where the water must be boiled for safety it is not uncommon to become bored by regular tea or coffee. An uplifting alternative is a long drink of lemon tea. A box of teabags (Lady Grey being my favourite here), a bag of lemons and a bottle of runny honey and you are in business for weeks. This recipe is also a great pick me up for those with colds or sore throats.

INGREDIENTS

1 cup (250ml) water
    per person, plus
    1 cup (250ml) for
    the pot
1 tbsp loose-leaf black
    tea per person, plus
    1 tbsp for the pot or
    1 teabag per cup
sugar or honey, to
    taste
lemon juice, to taste

METHOD

1 Bring the water to the boil, then add the tea. This can be loose-leaf black tea or a teabag of your favourite tea (Lady Grey or Earl Grey are very good, as is herbal).

2 Add the sugar and when dissolved, remove the pan from the heat.

3 Add the lemon juice.

4 Strain, as necessary, and serve.

TRADITIONAL *MASALA CHAI* - INDIAN SPICED MILK TEA

This is a wonderfully refreshing beverage that's equally good in the humid heat of the tropics as the chilly heights of the Himalayas. Across India, this *masala chai* is sold in small tea stalls, where you can witness a masterclass in its production. When making it for yourself, use whatever milk you prefer. If fresh spices are not at hand, dried ones can be substituted.

INGREDIENTS

Serves 4

2 cups (500ml) milk
2 cups (500ml) water
8 black peppercorns
4cm (2in) piece of
   cinnamon bark
8 cloves
6cm (2½in) piece of
   fresh root ginger,
   grated
6 cardamom pods
loose-leaf tea
sugar, to taste

METHOD

1 Mix the milk and the water in a pan and place over a low heat.

2 While the liquid heats, crush and grind the spices one at a time, adding each when ground to the milk. Add the ginger, cardamom pods, tea and the sugar.

3 Allow the liquid to boil and rise in the pan, then immediately raise the pan so that the boil subsides, then bring to the boil again.

4 Strain and serve by pouring four or five times between two pots from a height to aerate the *chai* before serving it.

QUICK-AND-EASY *MASALA CHAI*

Masala chai aficionados may throw up their arms in horror, but this fast beverage is pretty good and really suits lightweight hiking, where weight, space and stove fuel are limited. Powdered milk can be used in place of the evaporated milk. Powdered *masala chai* is also available but lacks soul. I prefer the teabag method as it retains a vestige of the drama of the street vendors' performance and you maintain control of the sweetening and milk component.

INGREDIENTS

½ cup (125ml) water
   per cup
⅘ cup (200ml)
   evaporated milk
   per cup
1 *masala chai* teabag
   per cup
sugar, to taste
   (demerara, if
   possible)

METHOD

1 Put water and milk in a pan with as many teabags as there are people. Allow about 1 cup (250ml) fluid per person, in a ratio of 3:2 milk to water.
2 Boil the teabags in the liquid for a couple of minutes, then pour into cups and sweeten to taste with sugar.

GINGER TEA

Ginger tea is another refreshing alternative to conventional tea. It is also helpful for settling upset stomachs. In the rainforest I have made a potent version using wild ginger. I like this drink in the tropics, it seems to aid acclimatisation.

INGREDIENTS

2cm (1in) piece of
   fresh root ginger
   root per cup
1 cup (250ml) water
   per cup
1 tsp lemon juice
   per cup
honey, to taste

METHOD

1 Peel the ginger, then slice into small pieces and boil in the water for 5 minutes.
2 Remove from the heat, add the lemon juice, then strain out the ginger and pour.
3 Sweeten with honey to taste.

COFFEE

One of the greatest joys of cooking is the heady aromas that emanate from the kitchen, a draw to the hungry and a torment to the satisfied. Who can resist the scent of a mirepoix rising from the pan or the enveloping perfume of freshly baked bread? But truly, is there any scent that can compare with that of freshly ground coffee? As I write these words, in front of me is a small leather pouch filled with freshly ground coffee. Despite the packaging, the whole pouch is gently scenting my studio with the allure of its dark, rich, velvety fragrance. It will not be long before I am compelled to put water over a flame and release the complex kaleidoscope of flavours from those enchanting ground beans.

Scents trigger memories: the scent of coffee reminds me of good friends and good times, but also some other things. During the dark days of the Second World War, Britain ran clandestine networks of saboteurs across occupied Europe. The agents who prepared to parachute into occupied Europe in support of these operations were specifically taught to pay attention to the aroma of coffee. For 'good coffee' was a telltale sign of black-market racketeering and with it the risk of being swept up in a crack down on illegal trading. Even the best forged identity papers were unlikely to withstand the resulting close scrutiny so agents were told to keep away from such establishments. When I raise a coffee mug, I often think of those courageous individuals who fought alone against tyranny

and despotism, many of whom selflessly gave their lives to secure the freedom in which I drink my coffee.

Brewing coffee outdoors

Making coffee outdoors is undoubtedly a ritual; one look at the pages of an outdoor equipment catalogue will quickly reveal that it has become a complex ritual. All manner of percolators and filters are available to be carried into the wild – many of them making relatively short journeys from production to landfill. Now, I am not going to say that these methods are inappropriate for coffee is an intensely personal thing. No, indeed not. But I *will* say that our reason to be outdoors is seldom just to brew coffee. In which case we should perhaps keep our methods simple and light.

I employ a range of different methods according to the way that I am travelling, all of which are a compromise compared to making coffee with the paraphernalia of a modern barista. But still, a very good cup can be made. The secret, if secret there is, is always to aim to produce a drink that tastes as good as the coffee smelled.

COFFEE BAG

On a day hike or when out watching wildlife, I usually carry only an army mug, water bottle and a spirit stove or solid-fuel stove with me, and that is perfectly adequate. With only the one vessel to both cook in and drink from, I use either a sachet of coffee (convenient, but worthy of no further discussion) or, more preferably, a coffee bag. The bag goes into the cold water, and just before it reaches a boil, I take the mug off the flame, let the bag brew for a couple of minutes more, fish it out and the coffee is brewed. Simple, delicious, job done! Now some may say it would be better to heat the water first and then to add the bag. Here I offer no resistance, save to say that my way is quicker.

DRIP-BAG COFFEE

If I am travelling light, camping out along the way and relying on a hike stove, I will certainly have with me a cooking pot or kettle as well as a mug. In these circumstances, I prefer to employ a drip coffee bag. I even make my own with my favourite Illy coffee. The drip bag is heat-sealed in a stay-fresh bag. Remove it from the packaging, unzip the top of the bag, then spread out the supporting cardboard wings on top of the mug. Now simply pour water just below the boil through the bag, being careful that it does not overflow. What a wonderful cup of coffee!

CAMPFIRE COFFEE – COFFEE ON AUTOPILOT

My favourite outdoor coffee is that which is brewed over my campfire. The fire lends its own smoky note to the coffee bouquet. Cooking coffee over the fire will, however, raise the eyebrows of coffee aficionados, who will be concerned at the temperature the coffee will be brewed. Coffee experts agree that the optimal temperature for brewing coffee is around 96°C (205°F). Modern coffee-making machines automatically regulate this. However, I can assure you that over the campfire we are not going to sit with a thermometer in the spout of our coffee pot. We are instead going to do the unimaginable and boil the water. Yes, this may burn the coffee and turn it bitter, but if we are careful in our method and the choice of our coffee, we can mitigate the negatives and brew a lovely cup of coffee.

When cooking on a campfire we need the correct coffee. Until relatively recently the Sami of Lapland, traditional campfire coffee experts, used to carry green coffee beans. They would roast these in an iron pot and coarsely crush them in a pestle and mortar or against a rock with the poll of an axe or the back edge of a *leuku* (knife). Today in Scandinavia, life is easier and it is possible to purchase special boiling coffee in the supermarkets. This is just coffee that has been coarsely ground. Coarse-ground coffee resists the high temperature of boiling water better than fine-ground coffee. It is easy to grind your own at home before setting out.

If you could be with me and my outdoor chums at a lunch stop in the wild you would witness us making coffee on autopilot. Whoever is nearest the resources kindles the fire, while another fashions the pot support. The coffee pot, dedicated solely to this one function, emerges from its sooty bag and is filled with clean water. Sufficient coffee is poured on top of the water, where it floats – there is no stirring. The kettle is hung directly over the flames, high enough that the heat is moderate. The moment the boil

is reached is announced by bubbles bursting free from the coffee, jiggling the pot lid. The coffee pan is immediately taken off the fire, swung and set beside it. There is no rush, no watching of the kettle, for as everyone knows, a watched kettle never boils. After a couple of minutes, we all grab our hand-carved cups and greasy sleeves wipe them. Now the coffee is poured out equally into each proffered cup. I am not going to profess that each cup is completely free of grounds, only that they are mostly so. We are not fussy outdoors, life is too short. The whole process is done on autopilot; no pontification or address is given to the pot or the company. It is straightforward and there is no fiddly filter to mess with or unnecessary coffee-making apparatus. The conversations of the company are enhanced by the informality of the coffee ritual. If we have been efficient, time allows and we are so moved, we may even hang the kettle for a second cup.

If the water is from a river or lake it should be filtered through tightly woven cloth, or a water filter, and then brought to a rolling boil for 1 minute. The pan is then taken off the heat and the coffee added and this time stirred with a convenient stick. It is left to brew for a few minutes in the warmth beside the fire or is raised high above the fire so as not to boil again. It is then removed and swung as before, and then served.

Quantity of coffee

This is a highly personal thing that depends on your personal preference and the blend and roast of the coffee you are using. Here is the best excuse in the world to drink coffee: go out and experiment. As a starting point, think in terms of 2 tbsp ground coffee per cup. I prefer to know how much is needed for each pot that I use.

In time, you will judge this by eye. Remember, coffee brewed strong can always be cut with water to taste. Attempting to rebrew with more coffee will spoil the first batch.

Settling the grounds

My preferred way to settle coffee grounds is to swing the pot at arm's length for two or three cycles. This centrifuges the grounds to the bottom of the pot. Give the pot a moment to rest after the spinning and then pour carefully. This is a highly effective method but requires a bail arm that is strong enough for the job. The last thing you want is to shower your friends with molten coffee grounds or to send your coffee pan into orbit. Alternatively, the pot can be tapped on its side with a stick. The tapping agitates the water and encourages the grounds to settle to the bottom of the pan.

Another popular method is to add a dash of clean cold water or a glob (1 tbsp) of fresh snow to the brewed coffee. The cold addition carries the grounds to the pan bottom. Some suggest using salt or egg shells for the same purpose – great ideas, which may work – however, one is a waste of salt and the other relies on having egg shells available, which is rare when travelling.

Coffee percolator

In my fixed camp I like to use a percolating coffee pot, whereby the coffee goes into a special receptacle inside the pot. When the coffee is brewed it can be seen bubbling through the clear pot lid knob.

Milk and sugar

On the trail, I prefer my coffee black without sugar, but let each person decide for themselves and act accordingly.

HOT CHOCOLATE: THE DRINK OF THE GODS

On an expedition there are times when no other drink will do. Hot chocolate is the ultimate morale-booster. What's more, the better the hot chocolate, the greater its comfort coefficient.

There are many ways to carry hot chocolate, from the original 100% cocoa logs and blocks, which are incredibly bitter and need culinary skill to handle, to all manner of powders and sachets, some of which include sugar and milk. These one-stop sachets are quick and convenient when using a hike stove but are insipid forgeries when compared to real drinking chocolate.

Real drinking chocolate

It is believed that chocolate has been drunk since at least 500BC and perhaps even earlier than that. The original Mayan recipe was a bitter, cold drink combined with spices, a far cry from the comforting beverage that we know today. It was during the late 17th century that recipes including milk popularised the product. During an expedition to Jamaica in 1687, Sir Hans Sloane encountered cacao, which was drunk locally mixed with water. Finding it distasteful, he is credited with introducing milk and thereby inventing the modern chocolate milk. By 1750, Nicholas Sanders, a grocer in Soho, London, was selling Sir Hans Sloane's Drinking Chocolate, perhaps the first branded drinking chocolate.

For real drinking chocolate, you need 100% cocoa chocolate found powdered, grated, in bean form or, as I prefer, a solid bar or block. The solid block must be grated, but occupies the least space, cannot be spilled by accident and, most importantly on an expedition, is more resistant to the greedy spoon.

DRINKING CHOCOLATE

This method is quick, efficient and minimises mess. Spices, such as orange zest or chilli, can also be added for a difference. At the end of a hard day's canoeing a tot of rum has been known to fortify a drinking chocolate, relaxing muscles and encouraging restful sleep.

INGREDIENTS

100% cocoa chocolate
water

milk, to taste
sugar, to taste

METHOD

1 Grate sufficient chocolate according to the manufacturer's instructions or your preference. Work to a volume of water of $2/5$ cup (100ml) for 2 cups or $4/5$ cup (200ml) for 4 cups.
2 Bring the water to the boil, then add the grated chocolate and when dissolved, stir into a smooth paste.
3 While stirring, add milk to taste and bring to the simmer, then taste and add sugar to your preference. If possible, whisk to aerate the drink before serving.

VARIATION

Milk powder can be added to the grated chocolate prior to the water. It can also be made without the milk if none is available. Evaporated milk mixed with water makes rich hot chocolate for cold weather.

RICE

The seeds of a grass *Oryza sativa* are the world's most widely consumed staple food. Better known as rice, this wonderfood daily provides one-fifth of the calories consumed by humanity and it is believed that it was first cultivated more than 10,000 years ago.

For travelling, rice is an excellent food: it packs well and provides a good energy yield. It is also tasty, easily cooked and a versatile accompaniment to a wide range of dishes and other ingredients. However, rice can be costly in terms of fuel so when travelling with a lightweight stove, quick-cook boil-in-the-bag rice may be the wiser choice.

Rice contains two types of starch: amylose starch and amylopectin starch. Rice varieties rich in amylose starch are those that cook well as loose-grained fluffy rice, while those rich in amylopectin are sticky and glutinous. Choosing the correct rice for your dish is important or, as may be the case when travelling in remote areas, choosing the dish for the rice that is available.

RICE SAFETY

Always make rice fresh and eat it immediately. Rice includes a gram-positive bacterium commonly found in soil and dust, *Bacillus cereus* – a bacterium that produces harmful toxins that can cause serious illness. In cooking, the bacterium is destroyed but not its more resilient spores. These begin to grow on the cooked rice at temperatures between 10–50°C (50–122°F), producing emetic and diarrhoeal toxins that are not destroyed by cooking. Outdoors, we do not have the luxury of refrigeration so we should time our cooking so that the rice is served hot within 20 minutes of completion. Any unconsumed rice should be discarded.

This bacterium is not just confined to rice, however: it will also grow on warm pasta, potatoes, meat, soups and sauces. A field kitchen should not contain cooked food just sitting around: cook it, consume it, discard the leftovers.

Rice falls into three categories:

1 Long grain rice – American long-grain white and brown rice, jasmine rice and basmati rice, white and wholegrain. These suit recipes that call for dry, fluffy rice. Also in this category is wild rice, which is not actually a rice at all but is harvested from aquatic grasses, *Zizania palustris* and *Zizania aquatica*.

2 Medium grain rice – Japanese sushi rice or Spanish 'bomba' rice are short and rounded. Bomba rice absorbs liquid well but retains its firmness so that when cooked, each grain remains dry, separate and fluffy. These virtues make it the legendary choice for cooking paella. It is often simply called paella rice.

3 Short grain rice – these rice varieties are creamy. Sticky rice from Thailand is very aptly named, while in Italy it is Arborio rice and Valencia rice that are the prime choices for risotto recipes. It's no surprise that pudding rice is also in this category.

VEGETABLES

Boiling is a convenient way to cook vegetables. When using a stove with a limited fuel supply, cut the vegetables smaller so that they will cook faster. When cooking dishes that contain a variety of vegetables, cook the harder, slower-cooking vegetables first.

While root vegetables will generally handle a long boiling well, more delicate vegetables are destroyed by being boiled for too long, losing their colour, texture and nutrients. Never boil any vegetable longer than is needed to cook it to the point of tenderness. To prevent overcooking, drain them immediately.

PERFECT PASTA

Pasta is a great outdoor staple – though almost never the fresh stuff since it has a short shelf life and needs to be kept refrigerated. Dried pasta, however, is ideal, being delicious, lightweight, easy to cook and having a long shelf life. Choose your pasta for its ease of packing: spaghetti, for example, takes up virtually no space compared to pasta shells or tubes.

HOW TO COOK PASTA

1 To cook pasta, bring a large volume of generously salted water to a rolling boil.
2 Add the pasta and stir it in the early stages of cooking to prevent it from sticking.
3 Boil for approximately 10 minutes. Once it is al dente – soft but still slightly resistant to the tooth – remove from the heat and drain.
4 If the pasta is to be combined with a sauce, do not add any oil as it will prevent the sauce from coating the pasta. If it is to be served without a sauce, drizzle a little good olive oil onto the pasta and toss to distribute and prevent it from sticking.

MEAT AND FISH

Boiling or poaching is a cooking method well suited to delicate foods such as fish, white meats and shellfish. Protein cooked in this way is rarely overcooked, does not dry out and usually retains its tenderness. It is a great method to use to introduce youngsters to cooking meat. At its simplest, the protein can be cooked in water, although with a little imagination this can be transformed with the addition of stock, herbs and wine.

HOW TO POACH CHICKEN BREASTS

Poaching is a great way to cook a chicken breast but is frequently overlooked. The meat can be cut into cubes or strips prior to poaching for speed or, as I prefer, cooked whole. Once poached, the breasts can be sliced and added to a sauce cooked separately, or shredded and added to a salad. In modern restaurants, this concept has been elevated to a new level in sous-vide cooking, whereby the water temperature can be maintained at a desired heat. Obviously, this is not an option in the camp, though!

1 To cook whole chicken breasts, skin and debone the chicken and then place the chicken breasts in a billycan large enough to contain the breasts without crowding them.
2 Cover with water or your poaching liquor so that they are well submerged.
3 Bring to a boil, then cover and reduce the heat to a low simmer and cook until done. Cooking times will vary with quantities of meat, volume of water and the ambient temperature.

HOW TO POACH FISH

Poaching is a brilliant way to cook delicate fish.

1 Begin by preparing your poaching liquor – this could be water or you could add a finely chopped shallot, some julienned carrot, finely diced celery, a sprig of thyme and 2 cloves.
2 Bring the liquor to a very gentle simmer and add some acid. This could be lemon juice, wine or even white wine vinegar.
3 Now take a fillet of fish – for example, trout – and place it gently in the poaching liquor, skin side down. It will only take few minutes to cook and will be opaque and flake easily when probed with the tip of a knife when it is ready.
4 Very carefully slide a fish slice under the fillet and lift it onto a plate.
5 Some of the vegetables can be removed from the liquor with a slotted spoon and added to the fillet as a simple garnish.

above Pike, filleted to remove all the bones – here using a paddle as a cutting board.

EGGS

Eggs and how to poach or boil them: I cannot count the number of times I have heard breakfast debates circle around these topics. It seems that everyone has a method, or at least an opinion. The secret, if secret there is, is to understand that an egg comprises three different types of protein: 1) the yolk, around which is 2) the thick egg white, around which, in turn, is 3) the thin egg white. Each of these layers contains different proportions of protein and hence each will set at a different temperature: the thick white at 60°C (140°F), the yolk at 65°C (149°F) and the thin white at 70°C (158°F). From this we can determine that to boil an egg with a runny yolk we must introduce the egg to high heat immediately so that the outer layer cooks before the core reaches its setting temperature. A hard-boiled egg can follow the same process but be cooked for longer. Alternatively, hard-boiled eggs can be brought to the boil with the water and will then require a shorter cooking time – around 7 minutes.

HOW TO SOFT-BOIL AN EGG

For what it's worth, here is my contribution to the timeless debate about how to achieve the perfect soft-boiled egg.

1 Bring a large billycan of water to a rolling boil. While the water is heating, place the eggs in a warm place, where they will reach body temperature.
2 Plunge the eggs into the boiling water and boil for long enough to attain the firmness you desire (see the table opposite).

3 As soon as the cooking time is reached, fish the eggs out with a slotted spoon and plunge them momentarily into cold water to arrest the cooking.
4 Allow the water to regain a rolling boil before cooking another batch.

Points to note:

- A large volume of water maintains its temperature better than a small volume.
- You may need to adjust the timing to suit other variables, such as the dimensions of the eggs and the ambient conditions.
- At altitude, water boils at a lower temperature and eggs will cook more slowly.

Egg cooking calculator

MINUTES IN BOILING WATER	FIRMNESS
4	very runny
5	thick runny
6	just liquid
7	soft boiled
8	softly set
9	firm
10	hard-boiled

Use this table as a starting point and you will not be far off achieving your perfect egg.

HOW TO POACH AN EGG

To my mind, a well-poached egg represents the very quintessence of cooking. Peer into the glossy yolk and you will discover the chef's respect for their ingredients, an understanding of food chemistry and the chef's personal skill.

It is such a simple, elegant offering – wonderful on its own, but it cannot be denied that it is elevated to a higher calling with the addition of some Hollandaise Sauce (see page 264). Yet, simple as it may be, many enthusiastic chefs struggle to cook this culinary marvel. Here is the process to follow to ensure perfect results. Now all that's needed is some practice.

1 Heat the water to a gentle simmer; a rolling boil will disturb the egg and make it difficult to manage tidily. If cooking many eggs, use a large volume of water.
2 To the water add plenty of salt and vinegar (salt 8g/litre and vinegar 15g/litre). This will help the egg white to set.
3 Stir the water into a swirl and carefully pour the egg into the centre of the vortex. The egg will sink to the bottom of the pan.
4 After 3–4 minutes the egg will rise up to the surface, where it can be fished out with a slotted spoon.

Points to note:
- Choose very fresh eggs. These have less thin white and are much easier to cook.
- A skilled chef can still manage with an older egg, but it requires a higher level of culinary dexterity. If you have a sieve, break the egg into it to separate the thin white from the thick white.

BOILED PUDDINGS

In home cooking, boiled puddings have fallen by the wayside. They seem old-fashioned and unsophisticated, but they were once a common part of cooking, for both sweet and savoury dishes. Outdoors in a fixed camp, however, they have lost none of their charm and will delight a hungry crew. This is real comfort cooking, ideal for the chill end of a spring or autumn day outdoors.

One of the best features of boiled puddings is that so long as the water is not allowed to boil dry, it is virtually impossible to overcook them. For a camp cook, the boiled pudding goes on first, allowing plenty of time to attend to the main course. Be sure to provide custard (see page 267), cream or evaporated milk to accompany them.

STEAMING

Steaming as a cooking method is frequently overlooked in the outdoor kitchen despite the fact that it has much to recommend it: steaming is well suited to the cooking of vegetables, delicate fish, shellfish and meats. Vegetables in particular respond well to steaming, cooking without loss of their texture, colour or sweetness and, like all steamed foods, they retain their minerals and vitamins better than when boiled. What's more, as an added bonus, steaming requires the use of far less water.

STEAMING FRESH FOODS

In the home kitchen, steaming is usually achieved with a dedicated basket or steaming vessel. Outdoors, though, it is easy to improvise a steamer: all that is necessary is a billycan with a lid in which the food is elevated above a shallow layer of boiling water and steamed with the lid on. **Cooking times will be slightly longer than when boiling.**

SIMPLE STEAM BAKING

Steam baking is a great way to break the monotony of boiled food when using a hiking stove. Steam baking cooks foods such as simple cakes and breads more quickly than dry baking, so requires less fuel, and it is also difficult to burn the food. The trade-off is that no crust is produced, but that is a small price to pay for the saving in fuel.

To do it, place a small pot inside a larger one with its lid on. A gap between the two pans can be achieved with three pebbles. Done in this way, small-scale steam baking can be very satisfying.

STEAMING IN A DOUBLE BOILER RIG

If you have billycans that are of the correct size, a double boiler can easily be used to steam more ambitious puddings over a campfire. For this, you will need a large billycan and a smaller one. The sizes are important: the small billycan with its lid on must sit inside the larger one with its lid on, floating on the water heated in the larger pan.

This is a really useful cooking method in windy weather when normal baking is difficult due to the uneven temperature on different sides of the pan. Here, the steam provides a more reliable even temperature throughout the vessel, although it is still wise to periodically rotate the pan during the cooking process.

POTATO SOUP

This is a wonderful earthy and filling soup, real comfort food, perfect on a cold day. The magic of this soup is the ease and speed with which it can be made. What's more, while it's a great soup in its own right, it can also be made with the addition of other ingredients, such as mushrooms, cooked sausage, fish etc.

INGREDIENTS

Serves 6

1 large onion
3 celery stalks
2 large potatoes
2 tbsp olive oil
1 tbsp fresh thyme
　　leaves or 1 tsp dried
　　thyme
4 cups (1 litre)
　　vegetable stock
　　(see page 259), plus
　　extra for thinning,
　　if necessary
salt and ground black
　　pepper
chopped fresh parsley,
　　to garnish (optional)

METHOD

1 Peel and finely dice the onion, then finely dice the celery and potatoes.

2 Heat the oil in a deep pan over a medium heat, then add the onion and celery and fry for about 15 minutes or until soft and translucent.

3 Add the potato and thyme, then stir in the stock. Bring to a gentle simmer, cover and cook for 30 minutes.

4 Blend with a whisk, then thin with stock if it's too thick. Season to taste.

5 Serve garnished with chopped fresh parsley, if you have some.

WATERCRESS SOUP

Watercress is often encountered on expeditions, so it is only natural to include a watercress soup. Be sure to be able to differentiate between wild watercress and fool's watercress (which tastes like carrot). Never gather either from areas where there are cattle or livestock, as they may harbour liver fluke. The method can be applied to many other edible wild greens, from stinging nettles and fat hen to sea beet.

INGREDIENTS

Serves 4

300g watercress
3 shallots or
    1 medium onion
4 celery stalks
3 tbsp olive oil
2 tbsp plain flour
1 cup (250ml) milk
1 cup (250ml) water
salt and ground black
    pepper, to taste
freshly grated nutmeg
    and a squeeze of
    lemon juice, to
    finish

METHOD

1 Remove and discard the stalks from the watercress, reserving the leaves.
2 Peel the shallots or onion, then finely dice. Finely dice the celery.
3 Heat the oil over a medium heat, then add the shallots or onion and celery and cook for about 15 minutes, until soft and golden.
4 Add the flour and stir; cook to form a white roux.
5 Gradually add the milk and water and stir in, then simmer and whisk until smooth.
6 In a separate pan, bring some water to a rolling boil, then add the watercress leaves and blanch for 1 minute. Immediately drain and cool with cold water. This will preserve the beautiful green colour of the watercress.

7 Drain again and cross-chop the watercress leaves into a puree, then add to the soup base.
8 Season to taste, then finish with some freshly grated nutmeg and a squeeze of lemon juice.

CARROT SOUP

Carrots are such a wonderful ingredient and go so well with coconut milk. The latter is of course also a useful ingredient for making Thai curries – it's well worth having in camp.

INGREDIENTS

Serves 6

1 medium onion
2 garlic cloves
2 celery stalks
4 large carrots
4 tbsp finely grated
   fresh root ginger
2 tbsp olive oil
4 cups (1 litre)
   vegetable stock
   (see page 259)
1 cup (250ml) coconut
   milk
juice and grated rind
   of 2 limes
salt and ground black
   pepper, to taste

METHOD

1 Peel the onion and garlic, then very finely dice them and the celery.
2 Peel the carrots, then shave into thin ribbons with a peeler. Cross-chop until very fine.
3 Heat the oil, then add the onions and celery and sweat for about 15 minutes, until golden.
4 Add the carrot and garlic and sweat for 5 minutes more.
5 Add the grated ginger along with the vegetable stock.
6 Simmer the soup for 20 minutes and then puree as best you are able with a whisk or potato masher. Do not worry if this is not possible.
7 Thicken the soup with coconut milk to preference.
8 Finally, add the lime juice and zest, and seasoning to taste.

Cook's tip
Using a weak stock solution prevents the stock from overpowering the fresh ingredients. I prefer low-salt stock for this recipe.

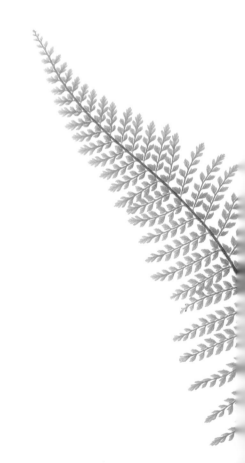

FRENCH ONION SOUP

A timeless classic that's easy to make in camp, the challenge comes from finding a way to toast the bread and cheese. I often delegate that task to another member of the party. It can be fun seeing how the challenge is met...

INGREDIENTS

Serves 4

2 medium onions
2 garlic cloves
2 tbsp olive oil
1 tbsp maple sugar or
  1 tsp sugar
2 tbsp balsamic
  vinegar
2 sprigs of thyme
2 bay leaves
splash of wine or
  brandy (optional)
4 cups (1 litre) beef
  stock (see page 262)
salt and ground black
  pepper, to taste
toasted French bread
  with melted cheese
  on top, to serve

METHOD

1 Peel and halve the onions, then slice thinly into crescents. Peel and finely chop the garlic.

2 Heat the olive oil over a medium heat, then add the onions and garlic and cook for about 20 minutes or until very soft and beginning to brown. Be careful not to let them burn.

3 Add the maple syrup or sugar and the balsamic vinegar, stir, then continue cooking gently until the onions are nicely browned.

4 Add the thyme and bay leaves. If you have some alcohol, such as wine or brandy, deglaze the pan to lift all of the reduced juices. Failing the luxury of alcohol, deglaze the pan with a little stock, being sure to lift all of the reduced onion into the developing sauce.

5 Add the rest of the stock and season to taste. Bring to the simmer, then cook for 20 minutes.

6 Traditionally, the soup is served with two slices of toasted French bread with melted cheese on top. If that proves impossible, just serve it with some bread.

NAKKISOPPA - FINNISH HOT DOG SOUP

This is one of the quickest and easiest of all soups to cook. It's very filling and satisfying – a great dish for a group. Serve with crackerbreads and some cheese.

INGREDIENTS

Serves 8

2 medium potatoes
1 onion
1 carrot
1 celery stalk
1 parsnip
½ swede
4 cups (1 litre)
  vegetable stock (see
  page 259) or beef
  stock (see page 262)
1 bay leaf
4 black peppercorns
1 star anise
6 hot dog sausages
salt and ground black
  pepper, to taste

METHOD

1 Peel (as required) and chop all of the vegetables into 2cm (1in) chunks.
2 Bring the stock to a simmer, then add the bay leaf, black peppercorns, star anise and all of the chopped vegetables.
3 Cook until the vegetables are cooked but not too soft.
4 Slice the hot dog sausages into 2cm (1in) lengths. Add to the soup, then remove the pan from the heat or, in cold weather, place over a low heat.
5 Cover and leave to rest for five minutes, then season to taste and serve.

CHICKEN NOODLE SOUP

Tasty and filling, this lovely soup is a perennial favourite that nearly always results in people coming back for seconds. Do not add too many noodles – they expand more than you may anticipate!

INGREDIENTS

Serves 6

2–3 chicken breasts
4 cups (1 litre) chicken
    stock (see page 261)
2 medium onions
3 large carrots
3 celery stalks
3 garlic cloves
2 tbsp olive oil
sprig of thyme
3 bay leaves
⅘ cup (200ml) wine
    (optional)
handful of a green
    vegetable, such as
    spinach or an edible
    wild alternative.
1 tsp honey (optional)
egg noodles,
    preferably whole-
    wheat
salt and ground black
    pepper, to taste

METHOD

1 Poach the chicken breasts gently in half of the chicken stock for 20 minutes or until tender.
2 Meanwhile, peel and then dice the onions and carrots and dice the celery. Peel and finely chop the garlic.
3 Heat the oil, then add the onions and celery and sweat for about 15 minutes, until soft and translucent.
4 Add the carrot, garlic, thyme and bay leaves and sweat for another 5 minutes.
5 Add the wine, if using, then add the remaining stock and bring to a simmer.

6 Remove the chicken breasts and retain the poaching stock.
7 Shred the chicken breasts with two forks and add to the vegetables, then add the reserved stock to the main soup and bring back to a simmer.
8 Roughly chop the green veg and add to the soup.
9 Taste the soup and adjust the seasoning: if it's bitter, add honey.
10 Finally, chop or break the noodles in half and add them to the soup. Remove from the heat and allow the noodles to soften – approximately 5 minutes.

SALMON SOUP

This is a classic way to make a delicious soup from stock. What I really like about this soup is that I literally use every part of the salmon nothing is wasted. Salmon is such a flavourful fish, ideal for this soup, but of course the same method can be used for all manner of fish varieties.

INGREDIENTS

Serves 6

Bones and trimmings
 of whole salmon
bouquet garni (see
 page 43) or whatever
 wild herbs are
 available
2 tbsp butter or olive
 oil
1 small bacon rasher,
 finely diced or 1
 small onion, peeled
 and finely chopped
2 tbsp plain flour
2 cups (500ml) milk
 or double cream
salt and ground black
 pepper, to taste
handful of finely
 chopped dill or
 crow garlic stems,
 to garnish

METHOD

1 Take the bones, fins and head filleted from the salmon, place them in a cooking pot and cover with cold water. Add the bouquet garni or herbs.

2 Bring to a simmer and simmer gently for 30 minutes, then remove from the heat and strain out the bones, reserving the stock.

3 In a second pan, melt the butter or oil and add the finely diced bacon or onion, then cook gently until softened.

4 Add the flour and stir. Keep the mixture moving and do not let it burn. Cook the flour through until it loses its floury taste and develops a characteristic nutty aroma, but do not let the roux darken.

5 Whisk in the salmon stock and milk or cream, then simmer for 10 minutes.

6 Season to taste. If available, garnish with a handful of finely chopped dill or crow garlic stems before serving.

SPICY TOMATO SOUP

This is my mother's recipe: an absolutely wonderful soup. If the tomatoes are bitter, be prepared to add a little sweetening. Serve with fresh crusty bread.

INGREDIENTS

Serves 6

1 medium onion
1 medium leek
1 celery stalk
1 small carrot
1 fresh chilli
2 tbsp olive oil
2 tbsp tomato puree
1 tsp paprika
1 tsp sugar (optional)
400g (15oz) can of
   tomatoes or 6 fresh
   tomatoes, chopped
4 cups (1 litre) chicken
   stock (see page 261)
salt and ground black
   pepper, to taste

METHOD

1 Peel (as necessary) and finely chop the onion, leek, celery and carrot. Seed and finely chop the chilli.

2 Heat the oil in a large pan, then add the onion and cook for 5–10 minutes, until soft but not coloured, stirring occasionally.

3 Add the carrot, leek and celery and continue to cook for a further 5–10 minutes.

4 Add the tomato puree and stir in, then add the paprika, chilli, sugar (if using), tomatoes, stock and seasoning.

5 Simmer gently for 40 minutes, then taste and adjust the seasoning to taste, adding a little extra sugar if necessary.

MUSHROOM SOUP

This earthy soup is made by combining a flavoursome mushroom stock with a béchamel sauce. The latter is made by blending a roux with some milk and is an incredibly useful beginning to a wide range of recipes. A velouté is made in the same way, except with stock in place of the milk – as in Salmon Soup (see page 172).

INGREDIENTS

Serves 6

2 shallots
1 garlic clove
250g mushrooms
2 cups (500ml)
   chicken stock (see
   page 261), vegetable
   stock (see page 259)
   or mushroom stock
   (see page 259)
2 tbsp olive oil
1 bay leaf
sprig of thyme
2 tbsp butter or olive
   oil
2 tbsp plain flour
2 cups (500ml) milk
salt and pepper

METHOD

1 Peel and very finely chop the shallots and garlic. Wipe the mushrooms clean and slice them finely.

2 Prepare the stock. To avoid overpowering the mushrooms' delicate flavour, I mix a weaker-than-usual stock.

3 Heat the oil, then add the shallots and garlic and sweat down for about 10 minutes, until translucent.

4 Add the bay leaf, thyme and mushrooms with a pinch of salt and some pepper and cook until the mushrooms are developing colour. As they cook, they will release moisture. Continue cooking until this has mostly evaporated.

5 Add the stock and bring to a simmer.

6 To give the soup its body, in a separate pan make a roux with the butter or oil and flour, cooking the flour until it develops a nutty aroma, but don't let the roux darken.

7 Carefully whisk the milk into the roux until a smooth sauce is created.

8 To combine the two halves of the soup, I whisk one-third of the mushroom reduction into the béchamel a cup at a time to ensure a smooth mix, and then add this thinned béchamel to the mushroom stock. If you need to thin the soup more, add a little extra stock or milk as your taste dictates.

9 Cook for a further 5–10 minutes, then season to taste and serve.

VARIATIONS

■ A few dried wild mushrooms can be very finely chopped and added to the pan in Step 5.
■ A cup of white wine can be added at the end of Step 4 and allowed to reduce by half.

VENISON SOUP

Soups can be tailored to suit vegetarian, vegan and vegequarian tastes, but we must not forget the delights of hunter's soups if meat is on the menu. This one features an Espagnole – a rich, full-bodied brown sauce made from browned roux, a brown stock and a few other ingredients. Here, it creates a hearty and filling soup that will pierce the chill of the coldest day.

INGREDIENTS

Serves 6

1 onion
2 carrots
2 celery stalks
250g (9oz) venison shoulder or joint meat pieces
4 cups (1 litre) beef stock (see page 262)
4 tbsp olive oil or butter
4 tbsp flour
1 tbsp tomato puree
1 garlic clove
1 bay leaf
2 sprigs of thyme
1 tsp allspice
salt and ground black pepper, to taste

METHOD

1 Peel (as necessary) and finely dice the vegetables.
2 Slice the meat into small pieces. Pour the stock into a pan and heat.
3 Heat half of the oil or butter in a pan, then add the meat and brown over high heat. Remove to a plate and reserve.
4 Put the remaining oil or butter in the pan, then add the onion, carrots and celery. Sweat for about 15 minutes over a medium heat until the onion is translucent.
5 Add the flour and cook, stirring to form a mid-brown roux.

6 Add the hot stock and whisk quickly into the roux to prevent lumps from forming.
7 Add the browned meat, tomato puree, garlic, bay leaf, thyme and allspice. Stir to combine, then simmer for 20 minutes.
8 Season to taste, then serve.

SAMI REINDEER SOUP

This uncomplicated soup reminds me of Sami friends and their closeness to nature: simple, functional, without unnecessary embellishment. They will choose meat with some fat attached for this dish.

INGREDIENTS

Serves 6

4 medium potatoes
1 onion
2 carrots
250g (9oz) venison
   shoulder
enough beef stock
   cubes to make 4
   cups (1 litre) stock
   (check packet
   instructions), or use
   fresh beef stock
   (see page 262)
1 tsp allspice
pinch of salt
1 tsp butter
1 tsp cornflour

METHOD

1 Peel (as required) and dice the vegetables and cube the meat.
2 Put the meat into a pan and cover with 4 cups (1 litre) of cold water. Bring to the boil and skim away any foam.
3 Add the stock cubes, along with the vegetables, allspice and salt. Cook until the vegetables and meat are tender.
4 Blend the butter and cornflour together to make a paste, then stir this into the soup to thicken it.
5 Simmer for a few minutes more, then serve.

NEW ENGLAND CLAM CHOWDER

A chowder is an essential soup for the outdoors as shellfish are so easily gathered on the coast and canned evaporated milk is convenient to carry. I always remember a Tsimshian lady explaining that 'When the tide is out, the table is set.'

INGREDIENTS

Serves 6

1 medium onion
1 celery stalk
2 large potatoes
1 tbsp olive oil or
    butter
1 tbsp plain flour
1kg (2lb) clams
    (see page 56
    for preparation
    instructions)
4 cups (1 litre) liquid,
    clam juice plus cold
    water
⅔ cup (170ml) can
    evaporated milk
sprig of thyme or 1 tsp
    dried thyme
salt and ground black
    pepper, to taste
finely chopped edible
    green leaves, to
    garnish
crackers, to serve

METHOD

1 Peel the onion, then finely dice that and the celery. Peel and cut the potatoes into rough bite-sized chunks.

2 Heat the oil or butter and sweat the onion and celery for about 15 minutes, until the onion is translucent.

3 Add the flour and stir to form a white roux. Add the clam juice or cooking liquid, along with the water, potatoes and evaporated milk. Bring to a simmer and cook until the potatoes are tender.

4 If necessary, mash some of the potato to thicken the soup, but ideally, the finished soup should contain a proportion of solid potato.

5 Add the clams to the chowder two minutes before serving. Garnish with finely chopped edible green leaves and serve with crackers.

MANHATTAN CLAM CHOWDER

This is my favourite coastal soup; even without clams it can be eaten as a stand-alone fish soup. Virtually any fish can be added, meaning it is a must for any outdoor group travelling on the coast or by boat.

INGREDIENTS

Serves 8

1 onion
1 carrot
1 celery stalk
1 leek
1 garlic clove
2 potatoes
2–3 bacon rashers
1 tbsp olive oil
2 tbsp tomato puree
sprig of thyme
1 bay leaf
400g (15oz) can
  chopped tomatoes
  or 4 large tomatoes,
  chopped

2 cups (500ml) fish
  stock (see page 260)
1kg (2lb) clams
  (see page 56
  for preparation
  instructions)
dash of
  Worcestershire
  sauce
salt and ground black
  pepper, to taste
parsley sprigs to
  garnish
crackers, to serve

METHOD

1 Peel (as required) and dice the onion, carrot, celery, leek and garlic. Quarter the potatoes. Dice the bacon.

2 Heat the oil, then add the bacon and brown over a medium heat.

3 Add the onion, carrot, celery and leek and sweat down for about 15 minutes, until the onion and leek are translucent.

4 Add the garlic and tomato puree, thyme and bay leaf. Cook for 2 minutes, then add the clam cooking liquid, tomatoes, fish stock and potatoes.

5 Bring to a high simmer and cook until the potatoes are tender.

6 Season to taste and add a good splash of Worcestershire sauce, then add the clams and cook for 5 minutes.

7 Season to taste, then garnish with parsley and serve with crackers.

PLAIN WHITE RICE

Quick and easy to cook, this delicious rice is a wonderful accompaniment to spicy foods and many sauce-based dishes as an alternative to potato. Try it with the Jägerschnitzel (see pages 114–15). Use a wide billycan with a tight-fitting lid wherever possible when cooking rice. This recipe is for 4 people, but scale it up or down, keeping the proportions the same: 1:2 rice to water.

INGREDIENTS

Serves 4

1 cup (175g) basmati
  rice
2 cups (500ml) water
1 tsp salt

METHOD

1 Measure out the rice into the billycan. Then, using the same measure, add precisely twice the volume of water and the salt.
2 Stir once and set over a high heat. Bring to the boil, put the lid on and raise the heat to a low simmer.
3 Allow the rice to cook for 12–15 minutes, then check on it. It should have absorbed the water and fluffed up. If it needs longer, replace the lid and check again after another 3 minutes of cooking.
4 Once cooked, lift the lid and fluff up the rice with a fork and allow any excess steam to evaporate before serving immediately.

PLAIN WHOLEGRAIN RICE

Wholegrain rice takes longer to cook than white rice, but it is more flavoursome and sustaining as a food. It's an excellent staple in a camp where expedition members have been working physically hard.

INGREDIENTS

water
wholegrain basmati
  rice
salt

METHOD

1 Bring a large pan of water to a rolling boil. Add ½ cup rice per person and a pinch of salt for each 1 cup of rice.
2 Bring to the boil, cover and simmer over a low heat for 25 minutes.
3 Test the rice. If it's nutty and tender, drain away the water and leave the rice covered for 2–3 minutes. If not, boil it for a few more minutes, then drain.
4 Serve immediately.

PLAIN WILD RICE

Not a rice at all, this grain has a deep earthy, nutty flavour and a rich dark colour that tastes wonderful alongside grilled salmon, roasted carrots and broccoli.

INGREDIENTS

Serves 4

wild rice
water
salt

METHOD

1 Add the wild rice to cold water in a ratio of 1 cup (175g) of rice to 2 cups (500ml) of water. Add a pinch of salt for each 1 cup of rice.
2 Bring to the boil, cover and simmer over a low heat for 45 minutes. It should have absorbed the water and fluffed up.
3 Test the rice. If it needs longer, replace the lid and check again after another 5 minutes' cooking.

VARIATION

If you prefer, the rice can be cooked in vegetable or chicken stock, in which case no salt needs to be added.

4 Once the rice is done, lift the lid, fluff it up with a fork and allow any excess steam to evaporate before serving immediately.

QUICK PLAIN WILD RICE

Pre-soaking overnight is the easiest way to cook wild rice. I have fond memories of cooking it this way in the camp of a Cree farmer who watched over a crop of wild rice in northern Saskatchewan.

INGREDIENTS

Serves 2

⅔ cup (125g) wild rice
1⅓ cups (300ml) water
pinch of salt

METHOD

1 Soak the rice overnight in plenty of cold water, then drain.
2 Bring the water to the boil, add the drained rice and a pinch of salt and give the usual cursory stir.
3 Bring to the boil, cover and simmer over a low heat for 20 minutes. Test whether it is ready. If not, give it another 5 minutes.
4 Once cooked, drain the rice, then cover and leave to rest 2–3 minutes before serving immediately.

NASI LEMAK – COCONUT RICE

This delicious rice is a wonderful accompaniment to curry, most especially the 'King of Curries', Rendang (see page 230).

INGREDIENTS

Serves 4

1 cup (175g) basmati
   or jasmine rice
1½ cups (375ml) cups
   water
⅔ cup (50g) powdered
   coconut milk
½ tsp salt
1 tsp sugar (palm
   sugar, if possible)
4 kaffir lime leaves
   (optional)

METHOD

1 In a wide billycan, combine the rice, water and powdered coconut milk. Stir to break up any lumps in the coconut powder.
2 Add the salt, sugar and kaffir lime leaves, if using.
3 Bring to the boil over a high heat, put on the lid and reduce the heat to a low simmer for 12 minutes.

4 Check on the rice and, if necessary, continue cooking for another 3 minutes.
5 Test again, then serve immediately.

STICKY RICE IN A PAN

Wonderfully glutinous sticky rice can be easily cooked in a pan.
I usually start the soaking at midday so that it is ready for the evening meal.

INGREDIENTS

sticky rice
water

METHOD

1 Soak 1 cup (175g) rice per person in cold water for a minimum of 4 hours, then drain.
2 Arrange a steaming set-up over a pan of boiling water.
3 Steam the rice, turning occasionally, until the grains are fluffy and translucent – usually around 20 minutes.
4 Serve immediately.

VARIATION

Alternatively, the rice can be rinsed three times and then cooked in twice its volume of water by bringing to the boil, covering and simmering for 12–15 minutes.

PERSIAN-INSPIRED RICE

Bejewelled with fruit this colourful, opulent rice dish is fit for the table of a Shah. I love to cook rice this way as it is easy to cook, provides added excitement and interest for a tired crew and is a great dish to welcome honoured guests to the camp.

INGREDIENTS

Serves 6–8

1 medium onion
1 garlic clove
4 tbsp flaked almonds
3 tbsp oil
½ tsp cumin
3cm (1½in) piece of
    cinnamon bark
2 cups (350g) basmati
    rice
6 tbsp dried fruit, such
    as sultanas, raisins,
    apricots
½ tsp turmeric
4 cups (1 litre) water
salt

METHOD

1 Peel and chop the onion and garlic.
2 Heat a frying pan, then add the almonds and dry-fry until just golden. Remove from the pan (to stop them cooking more) and reserve for later.
3 In a wide-based billycan, heat the oil, then add the cumin and cinnamon. When aromas are released from the spices, add the onion and garlic. Sauté for about 15 minutes, until the onion and garlic are translucent.

4 Add the rice and stir until every grain is coated in oil. Stir in the turmeric, add the dried fruit and stir to coat in the onion and spices.
5 Add the water and stir once. Bring to the boil, cover and simmer over a low heat for 12–15 minutes.
6 Check and test the rice, giving it a bit longer if it isn't quite done.
7 Once the rice is cooked, remove from the heat, fold in the almonds, cover and leave to rest for 2–3 minutes. Serve immediately.

VEGETABLE RISOTTO

Risotto is a wonderfully versatile cooking method that can be used to incorporate all manner of ingredients, including shellfish, fresh meat and even canned meat. Here, however, we've kept things simple and stuck to a few flavoursome vegetables and careful cooking to produce an ambrosial delight.

INGREDIENTS

Serves 4–6

4 cups (1 litre) vegetable stock (see page 259)
2 cups (500ml) water
1 onion
2 celery stalks
2 carrots
3 tbsp good olive oil
2 cups (350g) risotto rice
3 tbsp butter
2 cups podded fresh peas
2 tbsp finely chopped fresh mint
pinch of salt
2 tbsp grated Parmesan cheese
butter

METHOD

1 Bring the stock and water to the boil in a pan and maintain at a simmer throughout the cooking.
2 Peel the vegetables as required, then finely chop.
3 In a wide pan or frying pan, heat 2 tbsp of the oil and to this add 1 tbsp of the butter.
4 Add the onion and sauté for about 15 minutes, until translucent, then add the celery and carrots and sweat until soft.
5 Add the rice and sauté until just turning translucent. Add ½ cup (125ml) of the stock to the rice and stir gently. When the liquid has been absorbed, repeat the process. Do not stir vigorously or the rice will become too glutinous; just use a gentle motion with a wooden spoon or spatula.

6 Continue the process, adding a little stock at a time and waiting for it to be absorbed, until the rice is of the desired consistency. This will take about 25 minutes. The peas should be added halfway into the process, just as the rice begins to show signs of softening.
7 Once the rice has attained a creamy texture but remains slightly firm to the bite – al dente – remove from the heat, sprinkle over the mint and fold in.
8 Now add a pinch of salt, the grated Parmesan cheese and some small knobs of butter, and allow the latter to melt.
9 Give a final gentle stir, then drizzle with the remaining olive oil and serve immediately.

MUSHROOM RISOTTO

Meat and slow-cooking ingredients such as mushrooms should be cooked prior to being incorporated into the rice, as here. For the best results with all risottos, ensure that the stock is piping hot and stir gently and minimally.

INGREDIENTS

Serves 6

8 cups (2 litres) mushroom stock (see page 259)
1 onion
2 garlic cloves
2 cups mushrooms
4 tbsp olive oil, plus extra for drizzling
4 tbsp butter
2 cups (350g) Arborio rice
salt and ground black pepper, to taste
Parmesan cheese, for sprinkling
wild salad, to garnish

METHOD

1 Pour the mushroom stock into a pan and bring to the boil. Reduce to a simmer and keep it simmering throughout the cooking process.

2 Peel and chop the onion and garlic. Wipe the mushrooms clean and slice. Heat 2 tbsp of the olive oil and 1 tbsp of the butter.

3 Add the garlic and sauté for a few minutes, until translucent, then add the mushrooms and sauté until soft and nicely coloured. Remove from the pan and save for later.

4 Refresh the oil and butter in the pan, then add the onion and sauté for about 15 minutes, until translucent.

5 Add the rice and sauté until it starts to appear translucent.

6 Now add ½ cup (125ml) of the stock and stir gently. When the liquid has been absorbed, repeat the process. Do not stir vigorously or the rice will become too glutinous; just use a gentle motion with a wooden spoon or spatula.

7 Continue the process until the rice is of the desired consistency – about 25 minutes.

8 Fold in the cooked mushrooms, and, if necessary, add a pinch of salt.

9 Grate Parmesan over the top of the risotto, then add a couple of knobs of butter. Allow to melt, then fold in.

10 Grind over some black pepper, drizzle with good olive oil and garnish with some wild salad, wild bittercress, chickweed or even some freshly chopped wild marjoram – before serving immediately.

MASHED POTATO

Could there be a more comforting and satisfying addition to meat or fish dishes? The key is to make certain you leave no lumps in the potato, and to do this the potato has to be completely soft, and then left to steam dry before you mash it. The dish can be enhanced with a tablespoon of horseradish sauce, cheese or mustard. Mash with horseradish makes a wonderful topping for a Cottage Pie (see page 217).

INGREDIENTS

Serves 6–8

1kg (2lb) potatoes
    (Maris Piper or King
    Edward)
2 tbsp butter
about 1 cup (250ml)
    milk
salt and ground black
    pepper, to taste

METHOD

1 Peel the potatoes, then quarter and immediately place them into a pan of cold water to prevent them darkening in the air. There should be sufficient water to cover them.
2 Add 1 tsp of salt to the pan and bring to the boil. Simmer until the potatoes are tender when tested with a knife – about 15–20 minutes.
3 Remove from the heat, drain well and allow the steam to evaporate for a couple of minutes to further dry off the potatoes.
4 Mash the potatoes with a potato masher or even the end of a cylindrical section of green wood. As they start to become smooth, add the butter and a pinch of salt and pepper.

5 Continue mashing, adding a little milk, as necessary, to loosen the mash. Do not use too much.
6 Taste to check the seasoning and make any adjustment required, then serve.

CHICKEN *CHASSEUR* – FRENCH HUNTER'S CHICKEN

If I find fresh tarragon in the market my mind immediately thinks of this wonderful classic dish. Another rustic hunter's dish, it is quick and easy to cook, with a sauce full of flavour far above its humble simplicity.

INGREDIENTS

Serves 2

2 shallots
2 garlic cloves
8 medium
  mushrooms
1 sprig of tarragon,
  leaves picked
4 tomatoes
3 tbsp oil
2 tbsp tomato puree
2 chicken breasts
2 cups (500ml) chicken
  stock (see page 261)
4 tbsp cream or
beurre manié
  (see page 40)
boiled potatoes or
fresh bread

METHOD

1 Peel and finely dice the shallots and garlic. Wipe clean and then slice the mushrooms. Chop the tarragon.
2 Remove the skins and seeds from the tomatoes, then roughly chop.
3 Heat 1 tbsp of the oil in a pan over a medium heat, then add the shallots and garlic and sweat for about 10 minutes or until translucent.
4 Add the tarragon, mushrooms, tomatoes and tomato puree. Reduce until nearly dry.
5 Add the stock and reduce by one-third, finally thickening with cream or beurre manié.

6 Heat the remaining 2 tbsp oil in a frying pan until very hot, then fry the chicken breasts until golden on both sides and cooked through (the juices should run clear when pierced with a sharp knife).
7 Plate the chicken, pour over the sauce and serve with boiled potatoes or fresh bread rolls.

VENISON STROGANOFF

I like to make this dish with strips of venison back steak. The joy of this dish is derived from the combination of such wonderfully tender meat and amazing sauce. The secret lies in honouring the ingredients, do not overcook the onions and mushrooms, they should retain body. The meat will only need the quickest of cooking. I prefer to serve this with plain basmati rice.

INGREDIENTS

Serves 4

1 medium onion
good handful of
  mushrooms
1 green or red pepper
3 tbsp groundnut oil
⅗ cup (150ml) beef
  stock (see page 262)
500g (1lb) venison
  steak, cut into strips
water
1 tbsp Dijon or
  wholegrain mustard
⅗ cup (100ml) cream
salt and ground black
  pepper, to taste
Plain Wild Rice (see
  page 182) or boiled
  potatoes, to serve

METHOD

1 Peel and finely chop the onion, wipe clean and quarter the mushrooms and seed and slice the pepper into batons.
2 Preferably using a wok or a wide, shallow pan (to speed up evaporation and reduce cooking time, which keeps the venison tender), heat 1 tbsp of the oil and sweat down the onion for about 15 minutes, until translucent.
3 Add the onion, mushrooms and pepper and stir-fry over a high heat for a minute or so.
4 Pour in the stock and reduce to one-third of its original volume. Set aside the cooked veg in a warm pan.
5 Scrape out the wok, add the remaining oil and, over high heat, stir-fry the strips of venison. They should be brown on the outside but remain pink (but not raw) inside.
6 Reduce the heat and deglaze the wok or pan with a spoonful of water. Add the mustard and mix it through the meat.
7 Add the cooked vegetables to the meat, pour in the cream and bring to the boil. Season to taste.
8 Serve over a bed of Plain Wild Rice or with boiled potatoes.

POLLO ALLA CACCIATORA - ITALIAN HUNTER'S CHICKEN

By now you will have realised that I love hunter's recipes. So, this recipe is of course essential. As soon as the herbs hit the pan the aroma is wonderful, and you instantly know that something special is being cooked. You may need a long stick to fend off hungry diners drawn to the aromas. The recipe is also easily adapted to cooking rabbit. My wife's dear Roman friend, Barbara, insists that the recipe is improved with the addition of peppers, but I shall leave that for you to decide.

INGREDIENTS

Serves 4

3–4 garlic cloves
1 onion
4–5 sage leaves
sprig of rosemary, leaves picked
pinch of salt
1 chicken, jointed (see pages 224–5)
flour, for dusting
2 tbsp olive oil
2 tbsp tomato puree
1 cup (250ml) wine or chicken stock (see page 261)
handful of pitted olives
400g (15oz) can chopped tomatoes
water or extra stock, if necessary
salt and ground black pepper, to taste
3 cups (300g) cooked pasta bows or shells, to serve

METHOD

1 Peel and finely chop the garlic and onion. Chop the herbs finely and add a pinch of salt.

2 Season the chicken with half of the herb mixture and liberally dust in flour.

3 Heat the oil in a pan, add the chicken pieces and brown all over. Remove and keep warm.

4 Sweat the onion in the oil in the pan, then add the remaining herb mix and the tomato puree. Cook for a few minutes.

5 Deglaze the pan with red or white wine, if available, or use stock.

6 Add the olives and the chopped tomatoes. Return the chicken to the pan and simmer very gently for 20–30 minutes, until the chicken is cooked through and the sauce has reduced.

7 Season the sauce to taste and thin with water or chicken stock, if necessary.

8 Serve with cooked pasta bows or shells, or polenta.

VARIATION

CONIGLIO ALLA CACCIATORA - ITALIAN HUNTER'S RABBIT

The ingredients and method are the same as for *Pollo alla Cacciatora*, except that of course you use a jointed rabbit in place of the chicken. Add 6 juniper berries, partially crushed, in Step 4. Once the meat has been added to the sauce, increase the liquid by adding some stock to the sauce – perhaps as much as 4 cups (1 litre). It is not necessary to use all of the stock immediately – gauge it during the cooking. Wild rabbit needs to be cooked long and slow until the meat is nearly falling off the bone. Keep the sauce topped up with stock as it cooks, reducing the stock to the desired consistency at the end as necessary.

LINGUINE AI FRUTTI DI MARE – SEAFOOD LINGUINE

This is a classic recipe of Italian cooking; a perennial favourite made all the more special on those occasions when it is cooked beside the coast with freshly foraged ingredients. It is easily cooked with a hike stove amid the rock pools at the beach or on the deck of boat.

INGREDIENTS

Serves 4

4 cups (500g) mussels in shells
⅓ cup (100g) prawns
1⅓ cup (200g) cherry tomatoes
2 garlic cloves
400g (15oz) dried linguine
2 tbsp olive oil
pinch of chilli flakes
2 tbsp tomato puree
1 cup (250ml) white wine
1 tbsp lemon juice
salt and ground black pepper, to taste
sea purslane or 2 tbsp chopped fresh parsley, to garnish

METHOD

1 Scrub the mussels clean in cold water, removing any loose matter and the beards. Give each mussel a gentle squeeze to slightly open the shell. Discard any that do not close tight.

2 Remove the heads and tails from the prawns, slice along the backs and remove the black intestinal tracts. Rinse clean in water. Seawater is fine for these activities.

3 Slice the cherry tomatoes in half. Peel and dice the garlic.

4 Place the linguine in a pan of lightly salted boiling water and cook for about 10 minutes or until al dente (firm to the bite).

5 Meanwhile, in a wide billycan with a lid, heat the oil and cook the garlic, chilli flakes and the tomato puree for 2–3 minutes.

6 Add the wine and deglaze the pan. Immediately add the mussels and cook for 2–3 minutes with the lid on. After this steaming, discard any mussels that have not opened.

7 Add the cherry tomatoes and the prawns and cook for 3–4 minutes. Be careful not to overcook the prawns or they will toughen.

8 Add the lemon juice and season to taste.

9 Drain the cooked linguine, then add it to the shellfish sauce and stir in gently.

10 If you have been able to find some sea purslane, blanch a few sprigs in boiling water for a moment, then plunge into cold fresh water. Finely chop 2 tbsp and use to garnish the dish. Alternatively, use chopped fresh parsley.

SPOTTED DICK

An old English classic, spotted dick is real comfort food. While dishes such as this have fallen out of mainstream favour in the sophisticated light of modern food critique, their value and popularity, on a cold rainy day, remains undiminished for those living in tents.

INGREDIENTS

Serves 4

1⅓ cups (150g) plain flour
1 tsp baking powder
pinch of angler's salt (see page 52)
2 tbsp soft brown sugar
½ cup (75g) shredded suet or melted unsalted butter, plus extra butter for grease
⅓ cup (75g) sultanas
⅖ cup (100ml) milk
custard (see page 267), to serve

METHOD

1 Generously grease the inside of the small billycan with butter.
2 Put the flour, baking powder and salt in a large billycan. With a spoon, stir air into the mixture.
3 Stir in the sugar and mix with the suet or melted butter.
4 Once the fat is incorporated, fold in the sultanas.
5 Add the milk little by little to form a slightly stiff dough.
6 Place the dough in the greased billycan and put the lid on. Put the small billy inside the large billy and partially fill the large billy with water. Add the lid and place the large billy over the fire. Bring the water to the boil.
7 Continue cooking at a high simmer for 1½ hours. Maintain a watch on the water level to prevent it from boiling dry.
8 At the end of the cooking time, being careful of the scalding steam, lift out the small billycan and turn out the pudding onto a plate.
9 Serve with custard.

VARIATION

To enhance the pudding, sprinkle with brown sugar or drizzle with a tot of rum.

DEAD MAN'S LEG OR JAM ROLY-POLY

This classic steamed pudding was a favourite in the Kentish fruit and hop picking camps. It is a tasty and filling dish for those who have been working physically hard all day.

INGREDIENTS

Serves 6

2 cups (250g) self-raising flour, plus extra for dusting
¾ cup (100g) shredded suet
⅗ cup (150ml) milk
6–8 tbsp raspberry jam
1 tbsp sugar
custard (see page 267) or cream, to serve (optional)

METHOD

1 Place a large billycan or camp oven over the fire, then fill with water and bring to the boil.
2 Meanwhile, mix together the sugar, flour and the suet. Add enough milk to form a dough that can be rolled out and is not too stiff.
3 Roll the dough out onto a floured surface and with a floured rolling pin, roll into a rectangle with a width that's 4cm (2in) shorter than the pan's diameter.
4 Spread raspberry jam thickly across the dough, leaving the edges free of jam.
5 Roll the dough into a log shape, sealing the edge with a little water.

6 Scald a dish towel or similar clean cotton fabric, wring out the excess moisture and lay the cloth out flat. Liberally dust the top of the cloth with flour and place the roly-poly on top. Roll the pudding into the cloth and secure at the ends with a tie of butcher's string. Place two more ties around the body of the pudding. Do not tie tightly as the pudding will expand during cooking.
7 Plunge the wrapped pudding into the boiling water and leave to simmer for 2–3 hours. Check on the water level and top up as necessary to prevent it from boiling dry.
8 Fish the pudding out and allow to cool sufficiently to be handled. If it must be eaten immediately it can be cooled by quenching the wrapped package momentarily in cold water.
9 Serve with custard or cream, if you like.

PINEAPPLE UPSIDE-DOWN CAKE

This was the first type of cake I ever attempted to cook outdoors. It is so easy to make and always well received. Turn this out in the vestibule of a mountain tent when it has been raining for a week and you will be everybody's favourite chef!

INGREDIENTS

Serves 4–6

⅗ cup (150g) butter, softened, plus extra for greasing

1 cup (200g) sugar

227g (8oz) can pineapple rings, drained (reserve the syrup)

2 cups (250g) plain flour

2 tsp baking powder

3 tbsp milk powder

pinch of salt

2 eggs or equivalent powdered egg

water (see powdered egg packet)

custard (see page 267) or cream, to serve (optional)

METHOD

1 Grease the inside of the cooking pan well with butter (the pan should measure about 22cm/9in in diameter).

2 Mix 2 tbsp of the butter with 4 tbsp of the sugar, then sprinkle the mixture across the base of the pan. This can be heated and cooked until golden and caramelised, although I do not usually bother with this.

3 Place the pineapple rings on top of the sugar and butter. Reserve the syrup.

4 Mix the flour, baking powder, milk powder, salt and remaining sugar and butter. Add the powdered egg, if using.

5 Using your hands, combine this mixture well until smooth, then add the eggs if using fresh, or the right quantity of water if using powdered egg (check packet instructions).

6 Add the syrup from the pineapple rings and mix thoroughly with a spoon. Loosen the mixture by adding water as necessary until you have the consistency of thick batter.

7 Spoon this batter over the pineapple rings and spread evenly.

8 Place the pan into a steamer or double boiler rig (see page 161) and cook for 45 minutes.

9 Check if the mixture is cooked by piercing the centre with a skewer. It will be drawn out dry when the sponge is cooked.

10 Remove from the heat, rest for a few minutes and then turn out onto a plate.

11 Serve hot with custard or cream, if you like. It's also good served cold.

IN CAST IRON

I OFTEN WONDER HOW MANY OLD IRON COOKING POTS have been thrown away. Certainly, even when well cared for, a black iron pot will to the uninitiated seem an archaic relic of some ghastly culinary past. And woe betide the iron pot sporting a spot or two of rust when sitting beside clinically gleaming stainless-steel billycans. Despite their appearance, iron or heavy steel pots are perhaps the single most important and versatile cooking utensil in the fixed or vehicle-transported camp. Once you know how to use and care for one, you will quickly fall in love with it. These pots are amazing to cook in, holding heat and distributing it evenly like no other pan. This enables long, gentle stewing, fabulous roasting and, when it comes to baking, as you will discover in the bread section here, they are without equal.

CAMP OVENS

I like the term 'camp oven', it really captures the value of these simple cooking vessels. You may also encounter the term 'Dutch oven', a name that dates back to the 18th century when Abraham Darby from the Brass Works Co in Bristol patented a method for casting quality pots in iron – a method inspired by a technique he had seen used in Holland to cast brass pots. Iron, however, was a much more economical metal for cooking with. Even today, an iron pot is a good investment for when cared for it will serve many generations faithfully.

Throughout the 19th century, across the globe, camp ovens would serve families at the frontier of exploration and colonial migration. They hung from the frames of handcarts and covered wagons heading west during the great American migration, while similar iron *potjies* hung from the Voortrekker ox-wagons in Southern Africa. In New Zealand, in celebration of their worth, they were used in remote hunting cabins by government deer cullers and in the rugged Australian outback they were prized in the outback cattle stations. Today, ancient iron pots can still be found in the remotest cabins, some damaged or broken, serving only as rusty reminders of earlier times, while there are a few that are still cooking, their walls worn thin with care and generations of re-seasoning.

Today, camp ovens are still in use in the modern kitchen, mostly in enamelled versions by companies such as Le Creuset – wonderful pots that are more refined and delicate than the simpler camp oven used in a wilderness camp. Here, we can live without the enamelling and will look to pots designed to be used with embers.

Camp ovens come in many shapes and sizes; indeed, it would be a volume in its own right to even attempt to describe them all. The better foundries offer a wide range of camp ovens and the associated iron cookware and accessories. Some of these may even find good service in the home kitchen. However, tempting some of these items are, in wild places, weight and space are limited so we always employ the KISS principal: Keep It Simple Stupid.

With this in mind, the camp ovens we shall find most useful are round and cast with either a flat or round base.

FLAT-BASED CAMP OVENS

Camp ovens with a flat base are the most versatile and are a convenient shape for packing. They can be used for all types of cooking but really excel for roasting and baking. Consequently, this design is the most widely used. These ovens can be purchased with or without spike feet, usually in deep or shallow versions. Personally, I prefer shallow ovens without feet. For all their strength and weight, cast iron pots are vulnerable to being dropped or banged hard against solid objects. More than once I have encountered pots with broken feet. What's worse, quite often the foot removes a chunk of the pan base when it snaps off. Given that these pans will be loaded and unloaded from 4x4s, the feet are especially vulnerable. Also, those spiky feet have a habit of getting snagged on other equipment – and toes!

Camp ovens should have a strong bail arm for suspension. The lid should be designed with a lip or channel to hold embers as it will be necessary to cook with embers on top of the lid. A good lid can also be inverted and used as a frying pan. In some cases, the whole oven can be inverted, making a great pizza oven. The lid handle is also important. It should be tiny so that it can only be lifted with the aid of a hook or pot lifter; handles large enough to be grasped in the hand are an inviting temptation for forgetful hands. Iron holds its heat and when we are tired or distracted it is all too easy to reach out and lift a hot lid by such a handle. So, unless you intend to brand your hand with the maker's logo, opt for a small handle and a pot lifter. I carry a simple improvised pot lifter I made from fencing wire. It is also possible to make a simple wooden knob for a camp oven lid, which won't get so hot.

My favourite iron camp ovens are those made by Petromax. These meet all of my design criteria and have lids with sturdy tabular feet, enabling the lid to be inverted and used as a frying pan, and which allow several ovens to be stacked for cooking or storage. These ovens come in the following sizes: 1-litre, 3-litre, 4.5-litre, 6-litre, 9-litre and 12-litre, the most popular sizes

being 4.5- and 6-litre. Personally, I love the 3-litre camp oven; it is wonderful for cooking for one or two people and makes a great bread oven. The 4.5-litre will cook for up to four and is still relatively compact, while the 6-litre will cook easily for four to six people. The 3- and 4.5-litre can also be used in most home ovens. Clearly, the larger the oven, the more people can be catered for, and large camp ovens also allow for the roasting of whole legs and large joints.

ALUMINIUM

Camp ovens are also available cast in aluminium, which is much lighter. My first reaction to such pots was distrust, but in all honesty, they work very well and are a lightweight alternative to iron. Care must be taken, however, for in a very hot fire they could melt. Personally, I prefer my trusty iron camp ovens.

ROUND-BASED CAMP OVENS

Although the term *potjie*, pronounced 'poy-key', is strictly applicable to both flat- and round-based pots, it has become almost the universal term for round-based African camp ovens. Round-bottomed *potjies* are also highly versatile cooking pots and are nearly always equipped with feet as this conveniently removes the need for a support stand. If using a legless round-based pot, support it on three large stones or a round trivet.

The round-based camp oven has one great specialisation: long, slow-cooked recipes called *potjiekos*. Largely ignored by the world of fancy cuisine, it is a fact that *potjiekos* is one of the world's great dishes; almost every South African family has their own special recipe. Little beats the scent of such a meal mingling with the smoke from an African campfire. The sense of community and well-being that surrounds a *potjie* as the food is portioned out is quite unique (see opposite).

BEDOURIE OVENS: STEEL, NOT IRON

Iron camp ovens have to be cared for; despite its apparent strength, cast iron is brittle. If you drop a camp oven onto a rocky surface it can crack or even shatter. Equally, a hot oven quenched into cold water may also fracture.

During the 1920s, cameleers and cattle drovers in South West Queensland, Australia, frustrated by the number of ovens they had broken while packing across the rugged outback drover routes, asked a tinsmith in Bedourie to make an oven out of steel. Today, this has evolved into the spun-steel Bedourie Camp Oven and Aussie Camp Oven. Made from carbon steel, these ovens are much lighter than cast-iron ones and are virtually indestructible; I have a couple of Bedourie ovens that I have been using for well over 20 years. In many ways they are the perfect expedition oven: light, compact, tough and versatile. They cook differently to cast iron; being thinner, they cook quicker and it is best when baking to raise foods up off the oven base with a trivet. Like any oven, they require practice to master. I love mine: they are always there ready for the most demanding adventures.

POTJIEKOS – 'LITTLE POT FOOD'

Potjiekos was born out of hardship and hard travel and remains a wonderful way to cook outdoors; I love this way of cooking. In a fixed camp, the preparation can be done carefully with a cutting board and restaurant precision, while in a more mobile camp, the ingredients can simply be roughly chopped into the pot with a pocket knife. The spirit of the potjiekos is to combine whatever ingredients are to hand; there are no real rules excepting that the food is cooked slowly in an iron pot.

By legend, potjiekos had its origin in Holland during the 80 Years' War during the Siege of Leiden in 1574, when the besieged citizens survived by cooking whatever they could find in iron pots. At the conclusion of the siege, the famished townspeople rejoiced at the discovery of potatoes abandoned by the departed Spanish army and cooked a meal called hutspot, which is very similar to potjiekos and is still cooked today in Leiden to celebrate the event on 3 October every year.

When Dutch settlers arrived in Southern Africa, they brought similar pots with them. During the Great Trek, the potjie was an essential item of the Voortrekkers' camping equipment. At the end of each day's travel they would heat the pot and cook whatever meat they had or could obtain – impala, kudu, bushpig, warthog, rabbit, guinea fowl and so forth. To this they would add sections from large bones; the marrow fat melting from these would thicken the dish. Any available vegetables were also added and thus potjiekos was born.

Today, these dishes are often topped with starches such as pasta or rice. The method involves cooking the meal slowly over a low heat with little liquid so that the food steams. The ingredients are layered so that the ones that take longest to cook are nearest the bottom and those that cook the quickest are on top. The layers are not stirred so that they retain their individual flavours when served.

HOW TO WASH A CAMP OVEN

Camp oven aficionados state that you should never use soap to wash a camp oven. They are concerned that the seasoning will be compromised and give the impression that the oven can easily be ruined. Of course, this is not the case. I have always used a little detergent and a sponge scourer to clean my camp ovens. The detergent removes unwanted grease and keeps the oven clean. Immediately after washing, the oven is well rinsed, dried and oiled, so the seasoning remains intact.

However, I do not scrub vigorously, even when there are caked-on residues, which usually result from overcooking or cooking over too high heat. To remove these residues, I instead cut a piece of green wood to a chisel shape and scrape them off. They can also be burned off by inverting the pan over the fire, but I have never yet had to do this.

HOW TO SEASON A CAMP OVEN

Any camp oven – iron, steel, even aluminium – needs to be seasoned before use. This will protect iron and steel ovens from rusting and corrosion, but most importantly, it creates a non-stick surface in all the oven types, making cleaning much easier. Should the oven at any stage suffer neglect (most do) and develop a little rust, it can easily be cleaned up and re-seasoned.

You will need to take care not to burn yourself during this process. Use heavy-duty oven gloves and tongs as necessary.

1 Clean the oven thoroughly with a wire scouring pad.
2 Rinse the pot extremely thoroughly.
3 Dry the oven over a gentle heat.
4 Oil the inside of the oven with light olive oil.
5 Heat the oven until the oil begins to smoke, then remove from the heat and using tongs, wipe off the excess oil with kitchen paper.
6 Repeat the process several times until the paper towel emerges with excess oil but no black staining.
7 I usually give one more oiling at this stage.
8 Set the pot high over a fire to remain warm for several hours.
9 After every use, dry and oil the oven once.

USEFUL ACCESSORIES

Save your money for ingredients. You need only a few accessories for a camp oven. Most of these are also useful generally when cooking on an open fire.

HOOKS

Lifting a hot oven, raising a lid, sliding an oven away from the heat and a thousand other unforeseeable circumstances will require a pot hook. The hook could be whittled from a branch but will be better if it's made of metal.

For handling Bedourie ovens, I use a pair of long pot hooks. To lift lids, I use a hook made from heavy-gauge fencing wire, which is light and convenient. The hook must always be strong enough to handle the weight it will be lifting. Most foundries will produce ideal pot hooks and lid lifters.

GLOVES

With experience, it is perfectly possible to cook in camp ovens without ever needing to handle a hot surface, using a pot hook to lift and slide the pot as necessary. Nevertheless, it is a good idea to always have some gloves available. What's more, gloves are an essential item of safety equipment when handling cast iron. Choose heavy-duty baker's mitts.

TRIVET

A trivet is a three-legged support stand. Here, we are considering a trivet that can be placed inside the camp oven to elevate the food from the oven base. This can be achieved with a bespoke trivet or three stones upon which is placed a metal plate or mesh. I have even used hub nuts from a spare wheel – ideal as they are of identical height. (Just don't lose them!)

TONGS

A good set of lightweight stainless-steel food tongs is incredibly useful when cooking outdoors generally. When baking and roasting, they can be used to lift coals onto the lid of the camp oven.

SHOVEL

A shovel is not an essential item; it is usually possible to move embers with the aid of a stick or two. But since it is usual to carry a shovel for rescue purposes on an expedition, it can also be put to use moving embers. It does not need a long handle; if the fire is so hot that you need a long handle, you are almost certainly cooking with too much heat.

SUPPORTS AND TRIPODS

When I cook with a camp oven, I mostly suspend the oven from a tripod or place it on the ground surrounded by embers. It is also possible to carry a folding trivet to elevate the pot over the fire, although this results in the need for extra firewood to maintain the fire at a set height. A great way to support camp ovens is with two sections of angle iron supported in parallel on rocks or logs. These irons can easily be stowed in a 4x4 and if pans of differing widths are being used, they can be set closer together at one end to accommodate narrow ovens and pots.

HOW TO USE A CAMP OVEN

A camp oven is designed to be used over embers. Of course, it can be suspended over flames, but for the most part we shall be cooking low and slow, fully exploiting the evenness of heat the camp oven delivers. To achieve this, we shall heat the oven initially and then simply support its retention of heat high over the fire or, more reliably, nestled in a bed of embers, which can be refreshed as needed. My method is to rake aside the fire logs and embers and to place the oven directly onto the hot ground and to provide the heat to the oven around its sides by placing embers alongside. The fire is managed to one side to provide more embers as necessary. For stews and curries, I suspend or support the oven above the edge of the fire and manage the heat by adding or subtracting embers. It sounds complicated, but in practice it is not.

It is possible to use charcoal briquets to cook in a camp oven, but I prefer to use wood fire embers or locally sourced lump wood charcoal. Some like to dig a hole large enough to accommodate the oven, fill it with embers from a fire and then cook directly atop this ember bed. This method is reliable, although when baking or roasting in this way it will be necessary to employ a trivet within the oven to prevent scorching the underside of the ingredients.

Generally, there are two golden rules for successful camp oven cooking:

Do not use too large a fire. Cook with a moderate supply of embers raked to one side of the fire and refresh them as they become exhausted.

When baking with a camp oven, rotate the oven through 180 degrees every 15 minutes to ensure even cooking.

Lots of the curry, stew and soup recipes can be boiled or slow cooked in the oven, depending on time and other factors, though most will benefit from a long, slow simmer in the camp oven if that's an option. Baked foods, such as some breads, cakes and biscuits, meanwhile, are mostly designed for camp oven cooking. However, there is one cooking method in which they camp ovens truly excel: roasting.

ROASTING

One of the great joys of cooking with a camp oven is having the ability to roast foods. Just as for ground oven cooking, the roasting methods can be divided into wet and dry.

Roasting takes time. Perhaps the most common mistake made by enthusiastic wilderness chefs is to start their cooking too late in the day, which results in the meal being delivered in the pitch-black. Even with modern LED head lamps, in darkness it is difficult to properly judge cooking and simple tasks in the camp kitchen take much longer, only compounding the delay. The classic sign of this mistake is the camp chef peering into a camp oven and announcing loudly how wonderful and beautiful the food is. Nine times out of ten it is going to be overcooked; good food needs no announcement, speaks for itself and should be served at a time when it can be enjoyed, not when appetites have already boiled over and given way to thoughts of sleep.

While I generally avoid gadgets and fussy cooking paraphernalia, there is one gadget well worth including in the outfit for a fixed camp. That is a thermometer, to measure the internal temperature of meat being cooked. Not only can this reduce the risk of undercooking meat, but it also greatly aids the chef in serving the meat cooked to perfection. A simple analogue thermometer can be placed with its probe embedded in the centre of a joint while the meat is cooking. Alternatively, a digital probe may be used to measure the core temperature when the food is inspected. On page 258, you will find a table of minimum safe internal cooking temperatures.

POT ROASTING (WET)

Pot roasting is well suited to less tender cuts of meat or meat that is heavily marbled. A simple and easily controlled method of cooking, I favour pot roasting for inclement or stormy weather. It produces a one-pot meal; the joint will be roasted along with the vegetables, stock and seasonings.

The preparation, being simple, is very quick and the cooking is long and slow. Served directly from the pot, even in the worst weather the food arrives at the diner's plate hot – a hearty, delicious meal to warm even the most chilled campers. So long as the camp oven is checked frequently, so that it is not allowed to boil dry, it is hard to go wrong with a pot roast.

DRY ROASTING

Dry roasting is fussy compared to pot roasting but the results are spectacular. This is a special meal for a special occasion. For this method, the joint is elevated within the camp oven using a trivet. Part of the joy is in the presentation of the meal and the carving of meat slices from the joint.

This best suits more clement weather or else you run the risk of the meal being served cold. I experienced this first hand when I was once catered for in a Siberian bush camp in -7°C (19.4°F) conditions. Our Russian lady chef insisted each meal was served on a table. Lovely as the thought was, every plate arrived disappointingly cold. Her concept was sound and conformed to good manners, but she had failed to adapt to the weather conditions. A pot roast would have been much more appropriate.

POT ROAST BEEF

When the days are short, I like a good pot roast. The whole dish is prepared in a few minutes and everything is easily cooked in one pot. A camp oven is perfect here, like the small oven pictured here with a 500g/1lb beef joint. Only cook the meat until done, over cooking will cause it to become dry. Be prepared to thicken the gravy.

INGREDIENTS

Serves 4–6

2 medium onions
4 medium carrots
4 medium potatoes
4 tbsp oil
500g (1lb) beef
1 cup (250ml) beer
   (optional), or extra
   stock
1 cup (250ml) stock
   (beef stock is ideal,
   see page 262)
salt and ground black
   pepper, to taste

METHOD

1 Heat a camp oven.
2 Peel and roughly chop the vegetables – leave them chunky.
3 Heat the oil in the camp oven. When it is very hot, sear the outside of the beef joint on each of its sides to seal it. Remove it to a plate and season well with salt and pepper.
4 Place the onions in the camp oven and put the meat on top. Surround it with the carrots and potatoes.
5 Add the beer, if using, and the stock, then close the lid.

6 Cook over a moderate heat for 2 hours, until the meat is incredibly tender. Ensure that you check on the oven periodically to prevent it from drying out. Top up with water or stock as necessary.
7 Remove the meat from the pot and place it on a board to slice it. Serve with the cooked vegetables and some of the delicious gravy.

ROAST LAMB

This is a joy of the fixed camp in the spring or early summer. Lamb combined with garlic and rosemary is a miracle of the culinary kind. I use the same recipe to cook a haunch of venison. You will need two camp ovens though, as the diners will demand roast potatoes to eat in concert with the joint.

INGREDIENTS

Serves 4–6

1 medium onion
2 medium carrots
2 celery stalks
1 garlic bulb
leg of lamb
6 sprigs of rosemary
4 tbsp oil
2 cups (500ml) water
salt and ground black
    pepper, to taste
Roast Potatoes (see
    page 214) and
    cooked vegetables,
    to serve

METHOD

1 Place a trivet in a camp oven and heat the oven.
2 Peel and roughly chop the vegetables. Divide the garlic bulb into cloves and peel them.
3 Pierce the leg of lamb all over with the point of a knife to create pockets into which cloves of garlic can be placed, along with sprigs of rosemary. Rub the oil and then the seasoning over the whole joint.
4 Place the joint onto the trivet in the camp oven, surround with vegetables, then add the water.
5 Close the oven and cook over a medium heat, allowing 30 minutes per 500g (1lb), plus 30 minutes to finish. Check on the joint every 10 minutes and rotate the oven each time. Do not add any more water.
6 Towards the end of the cooking time, place embers on the lid of the oven to brown the top of the joint.

VARIATION

This recipe is also the perfect way to cook a haunch of venison. Deboned and rolled haunches occupy less room for storage and can be cooked in a smaller oven.

7 Once cooked, remove the joint and set aside to rest for about 30 minutes,
8 Meanwhile, remove the trivet and deglaze the juices in the pan to make Gravy From the Pan (see page 263). Carve and serve with Roast Potatoes and cooked vegetables, such as carrots or peas.

ROAST CHICKEN

If you are already an experienced outdoor cook then this dish needs no introduction. If you are just starting on the path of outdoor cooking, the roast chicken is the perfect dish to begin with as it is an easy, classic dish to serve.

INGREDIENTS

Serves 4–6

2 celery stalks
1 medium onion
1 medium carrot
1 lemon, halved and/
    or 1 onion, peeled
1 chicken
olive oil
thyme or marjoram,
    leaves picked and
    chopped
salt and ground black
    pepper, to taste
Roast Potatoes (see
    page 214) and roast
    or boiled vegetables
    or salad, to serve

METHOD

1 Place a trivet in a camp oven and heat the oven.
2 Peel and chop the vegetables.
3 Stuff the chicken with the lemon and/or onion.
4 Rub the chicken all over with oil, then season with salt, pepper and the herb of your choice. A seasoning spice mix may also be used. I like to use angler's salt (see page 52).
5 Place in the heated oven and cook over a moderate heat for 20 minutes, plus 20 minutes per 450g weight of chicken.
6 Towards the end of the cooking time, add coals to the lid to brown the top of the chicken.
7 When cooked, remove the chicken from the pan and leave to rest in a warm pan.
8 Remove the trivet, deglaze the juices in the pan and make Gravy From the Pan (see page 263).
9 Carve the chicken and serve with Roast Potatoes, vegetables or salad.

ROAST POTATOES

The ultimate accompaniment to any roast has to be golden roast potatoes. Quantities and the cooking time will of course vary according to the number of diners, their appetite, the size of the pan available and the weather conditions, so use your judgement.

INGREDIENTS

Serves 4

1kg (2lb) floury
   potatoes
   (King Edward
   or Maris Piper)
goose fat or oil
salt

METHOD

1 Peel the potatoes, cut them in half, then place them immediately in a large billycan of salted water.
2 Bring the billycan to the boil and simmer the potatoes for no more than 5 minutes, until just slightly tender.

3 Drain well, return the potatoes to the billycan and with the lid on, shake the pan vigorously to soften the outside surface of the potatoes. Remove the lid and allow the steam in the pan to evaporate and the potatoes to dry.
4 Put a camp oven over a moderate heat and melt the goose fat or heat the oil. You will only need sufficient fat to coat the potatoes – do not drown them.
5 Once the fat or oil is very hot, spoon in the potatoes and roll in it until covered.
6 Put the lid on the oven and cook for about 30 minutes. Every 10 minutes, remove the lid and turn and baste the potatoes. Removing the lid helps to release the steam in the pan, leading to crispier potatoes. Never crowd the pan with potatoes or there will be too much steam, resulting in cooked but not crispy potatoes.

YORKSHIRE PUDDING

Prepare the batter for the Yorkshire pudding while the meat is cooking, then cook it while the meat is resting. Rather than carrying a special pudding baking tray we shall simply make one large pudding and portion it out. This not only reduces the necessary cooking equipment, but it is also safer as we don't have to fiddle with a hot pan filled with hot oil in a hot camp oven.

INGREDIENTS

Serves 4–6

5 tbsp milk powder or about 1 cup (250ml) milk
4 tbsp powdered egg or 2 eggs
about 1 cup (250ml) water, if using milk powder and powdered egg
about 1 cup (125g) plain flour
4 tbsp oil or goose fat
salt and ground black pepper, to taste

METHOD

1   Whisk the milk powder and powdered egg with the water, if using, or whisk together the milk and eggs.
2   Whisk in the flour a little at a time until you have a batter with the consistency of thick cream. If necessary, relax the batter with a little water or add a little more flour. Add a good pinch of salt and pepper.
3   In a large pan lid or frying pan, heat the oil or fat on a trivet inside a hot camp oven. When the oil is just reaching the smoke point, pour in the batter and cover the pan

4   Place some embers on the lid. Cook for 20 minutes before raising the lid to inspect the Yorkshire pudding. Cover again and continue cooking until golden brown.
5   Remove from the pan with tongs and slice into portions.

CHILLI CON CARNE

This is always a favourite dish. For best results make the chilli early and keep it warm high over the fire so it doesn't dry out. The flavour develops well with longer cooking.

INGREDIENTS

Serves 4

2 medium onions
2 celery stalks
2 medium carrots
3 garlic cloves
3 tbsp oil
500g (1lb) minced
  beef or venison
2 tbsp balsamic
  vinegar
1 tbsp tomato puree
1 tsp chilli powder
1 tsp ground cumin
1 cup (250ml) red
  wine (optional)
400g (15oz) can kidney
  beans
2 x 400g (15oz) cans
  chopped tomatoes
2 tsp honey
salt and ground black
  pepper, to taste
Plain White Rice
  (see page 181) and
  natural yogurt
  (optional), to serve

METHOD

1 Peel and finely chop the vegetables and garlic.

2 Set a camp oven over a low heat, add half the oil and sauté the onions, celery, carrots and garlic for about 15 minutes, until the onions and garlic are translucent.

3 In a frying pan, heat the remaining oil and brown the mince in small batches, adding it to the sautéed vegetables as you go.

4 Mix well and stir in the balsamic vinegar, tomato puree, chilli powder and cumin. If you have some red wine available, add it at this stage, but this is optional.

5 Add the kidney beans and the chopped tomatoes and stir to combine.

6 Cook, covered, over a medium heat for 1 hour. The sauce should reduce and thicken, but do not allow it to boil dry.

7 Taste the chilli and season with salt and pepper. Add honey to relieve any bitterness.

8 Serve with Plain White Rice and, if available, natural yogurt.

COTTAGE PIE

This is a wonderful, hearty dish that's always popular, particularly at the end of a busy day. I once cooked this in the wilderness of Northern Australia after a particularly testing day's travel, when the mood in the party was tense with frustration. Delegating the preparation and peeling tasks gave discouraged minds new focus and allowed me to get on with making the fire just so. By the time our gargantuan cottage pie had been devoured, everyone was still tired but now cheerful and ready to share jokes that quite frankly should never have been remembered, let alone passed around the fire. Food really does have healing properties.

INGREDIENTS

Serves 4

1 onion
2 carrots
2 celery stalks
2 garlic cloves
2 tbsp oil
1 sprig of rosemary,
    leaves picked and
    chopped
2 tsp Worcestershire
    sauce
500g (1lb) minced beef
    or venison
1 tbsp flour
2–3 cups (500–750ml)
    beef stock (see
    page 262)
about 750g (1½lb)
    potatoes
2 tbsp butter
3 tbsp milk
salt and ground black
    pepper, to taste

METHOD

1 Peel and finely chop the vegetables and garlic.

2 Heat the oil in a Dutch oven, then add the vegetables and sauté for about 15 minutes, until the onion and garlic are translucent.

3 Add the rosemary and Worcestershire sauce, then add the mince and stir to break up any lumps. Cook until browned all over.

4 Sprinkle flour over the meat and stir it into the mixture. Add beef stock to the level of the meat and leave to simmer while you prepare the mashed potatoes.

5 Peel and chop the potatoes, then boil them in a pan of lightly salted water for 10–15 minutes, until soft. Drain well, leave to steam dry for 1 minute, then mash. Add the butter, milk and some salt and pepper, then stir to combine.

6 Spread a thick layer of mashed potato over the meat, then using a fork, create a pleasing pattern on the surface, with some little crests.

7 Put the lid on the Dutch oven and cook over a medium heat for 30 minutes. Finish off by lightly browning the crests of the potato by placing a layer of embers on the lid of the Dutch oven to give the top a blast of heat for 3–4 minutes.

VENISON BOLOGNAISE

Traditionally, Bolognaise sauce is cooked without herbs, but I must confess I love to add a sprig of rosemary at the vegetable stage of the recipe. The secret to a good Bolognaise is simplicity and a slow cooking of the sauce. The Dutch oven is perfect for this.

INGREDIENTS

Serves 4

1 onion
2 carrots
2 celery stalks
2 garlic cloves
few rashers of
    pancetta or bacon
2 tbsp oil
sprig of rosemary,
    leaves picked and
    chopped
2 tbsp tomato puree
500g (1lb) minced
    venison or beef
1 cup (250ml) red
    wine (optional), or
    the same volume
    of extra stock
2–3 cups (500–750ml)
    beef or chicken
    stock (see pages
    261 and 262)
about 300g dried
    spaghetti
salt and ground black
    pepper, to taste
grated cheese and
    chopped fresh basil,
    to serve

METHOD

1 Peel and finely chop the vegetables and garlic. Dice the pancetta or bacon.

2 Heat the oil in a large billycan or Dutch oven and cook the pancetta or bacon in it.

3 Add the vegetables, garlic, rosemary and the tomato puree. Cook for about 15 minutes, until just beginning to caramelise.

4 Add the mince and cook evenly until browned all over and all of the water has been driven off.

5 Deglaze the pan with a cup of stock or wine, if it is available. Add sufficient stock to just cover the meat, a good pinch of salt and pepper, and cook slowly over a low heat for about an hour, or more, to the consistency you desire.

6 Taste and adjust the seasoning as required.

7 While the sauce is reducing, add the spaghetti to a pan of boiling lightly salted water and cook for about 10 minutes, or until al dente.

8 Serve the spaghetti with the sauce on top, sprinkled with some grated cheese (Parmesan, if possible) and some chopped fresh basil.

Cook's tip
If required, the carrot can be grated with a peeler and then chopped very finely.

TOAD-IN-THE-HOLE

Sausages in a camp are normally pan-fried or cooked on skewers. But with this classic recipe they can be transformed into a more impressive hearty meal. This is such an easy dish, I am surprised it is not cooked outdoors more often. I like this as a surprise lunch in a busy camp, especially in cold or damp weather.

INGREDIENTS

Serves 4

about 12 chipolatas
   or 8 sausages
oil for roasting
4 tbsp powdered egg
   or 2 real eggs
3 tbsp milk powder or
   ⅘ cup (200ml) milk
about 1 cup (250ml)
   water, if using
   milk powder and
   powdered egg
about 1 cup (125g)
   plain flour
1 tbsp dried thyme or
   rosemary (optional)
salt and ground black
   pepper, to taste
Gravy From Scratch
   (see page 263),
   to serve

METHOD

1 In a large pan or billycan lid, heat the oil and roast the chipolatas or sausages in the oil inside the hot camp oven using a trivet, until golden brown all over.

2 Meanwhile, make the batter by whisking together the powdered egg, milk powder and water, or the real eggs and milk.

3 Whisk in the flour, little by little, until a batter with the consistency of thick cream is formed. Add a little more milk/water or flour as required. Season with salt and pepper and some dried thyme or rosemary, if you like.

4 After the chipolatas have been roasting for 15 minutes or the sausages have had 25 minutes, and are golden brown all over, pour the batter around them.

5 Cover the pan again and cook for a further 25–30 minutes, until the batter is puffed up and golden. Serve with gravy.

Cook's tip

If time is short, slice the sausages in half lengthways before roasting.

CONEJO A LA CAZADORA - SPANISH HUNTER'S RABBIT

This rich tomato dish is a delicious way to cook rabbit, a real celebration of the main ingredient. It works equally well with chicken. As with all dishes of this style, once the meat is browned raise the pot from the fire to a gentle heat and allow the sauce base to properly develop before the deglazing. A lovely dish for novice chefs.

INGREDIENTS

Serves 4

1 rabbit
6 garlic cloves
1 green pepper
1 large carrot
1 tbsp olive oil
1 bay leaf
2 sprigs of thyme
2 tbsp tomato puree
1 cup (250ml) red
   or white wine
   or chicken stock
   (see page 261)
400g (15oz) can
   chopped tomatoes
water
handful of green
   beans
salt and ground black
   pepper, to taste
boiled potatoes,
   to serve

METHOD

1 Quarter the rabbit and season it all over. Peel and finely chop the garlic, seed and dice the pepper, and peel and dice the carrot into 6mm (¼in) pieces.

2 In a large pan or Dutch oven, heat the oil and cook the garlic with the bay leaf for a few minutes, until soft but not coloured.

3 Add the rabbit and cook, stirring continuously, until browned on all sides.

4 Add the pepper, carrot, thyme and tomato puree and cook for a couple of minutes.

5 Deglaze the pan with a cup of wine or stock. Add the chopped tomatoes and water to just cover the rabbit.

6 Cook slowly over a medium heat for about 20 minutes, until the rabbit is tender and the sauce is reduced to your preference.

7 Finally, chop the green beans into 2cm (1in) sections and add to the sauce. Simmer for about 10 minutes, until tender,

8 Serve the stew with boiled potatoes.

VENISON *POTJIEKOS*

This *potjie* is a wonderful cooking pot to use, once you become accustomed to cooking with one you will discover that almost every ingredient has magic worked upon it by the pot. This simple dish is inspired by the *potjies* that swung beside the axle of the voortrekkers Ossewa (ox cart).

INGREDIENTS

Serves 4

1 large onion
4 medium potatoes
4 medium carrots
4 tbsp oil
500g (1lb) best
  braising venison
  (or use beef)
2 tbsp Worcestershire
  sauce or balsamic
  vinegar
4 tbsp chutney (Mrs
  Balls Chutney [if
  you can get it], for
  a more authentic
  South African
  flavour)
2 cups (500ml) beef
  stock (see page 262)
  or 1 cup (250ml)
  each of red wine
  and beef stock
6 medium
  mushrooms
salt and ground black
  pepper, to taste
crusty bread, to serve

METHOD

1 Heat the *potjie* over a bed of embers to a moderate heat.
2 Peel the vegetables, roughly chop the onion and cut the potatoes and carrots into bite-sized chunks.
3 Add the oil to the *potjie* and sweat the onion for about 15 minutes, until translucent.
4 Add the meat and stir until it is browned on all sides. Add the Worcestershire sauce or balsamic vinegar, the chutney and a little seasoning, then stir well through the meat.
5 Lay the carrot segments over the meat and the potato as a layer over the carrot. Pour over the stock.

6 Cover the *potjie* and cook very gently for 1½ hours. Check occasionally to ensure that the pot has not boiled dry.
7 Add the mushrooms and continue cooking for another 30 minutes.
8 Check that all the layers are cooked and, if so, serve with some crusty bread.

CHICKEN *POTJIEKOS*

A chicken *potjiekos* is a wonderful thing, so quick, so easy, so satisfying. You have not cooked outdoors until you have had a chicken *potjiekos*.

INGREDIENTS

Serves 4

1 medium onion
2 large carrots
4 medium sweet
  potatoes
4 tbsp oil
4 chicken thighs
2 bay leaves
1 cup (190g) dried
  apricots
2 corn on the cob
1 cup (250ml) chicken
  stock (see page 261)
  or white wine or
  Madeira sherry
salt and ground black
  pepper, to taste
Plain White Rice (see
  page 181), to serve

METHOD

1 Peel and roughly chop the onion, carrots and sweet potatoes while the *potjie* heats over a moderate heat.
2 Heat the oil, then add the onion to the *potjie* and sweat for about 15 minutes, until translucent.
3 Add the chicken thighs, skin side down, and cook until they begin to brown, turning twice.
4 Add the bay leaves, then layer the carrots over the chicken and the sweet potato over the carrots.

Sprinkle dried apricots over the sweet potato.
5 Cut the corn through into 2.5cm (1in) slices and place these over the other ingredients. Pour over the liquid.
6 Replace the lid and cook gently for 1 hour. Be sure that the *potjie* does not dry out.
7 After 1 hour, check that the ingredients are cooked. If so, serve with Plain White Rice.

HOW TO JOINT A CHICKEN

1 With the back of a knife scrape the flesh to expose the wish bone.

2 Cut through the end of the wish bone forks, then lever the wishbone upwards and it will part easily from the body.

3 At the mid-point cut around the first wing bone.

4 Scrape away the flesh from the bone towards the elbow joint.

5 Scraped well the joint will separate easily and neatly. Remove the wing tip at the obvious joint.

6 Spread the legs out one at a time stretching the skin and slice to leave as much skin as possible on the breast.

7 Follow the natural line between the muscles to the ball joint, sever the connecting tendon and remove the leg.

8 Cut through the natural join of the first leg joint.

9 Feel for the hidden knee joint and cut cleanly through it to separate drumstick from thigh.

10 Done well the drumstick will look like this.

11 Expose the thigh bone with the tip of the knife and remove it.

12 Cutting as close to the bone as possible, carefully slice either side of the breastbone to remove the breasts.

Done correctly there are eight prime pieces: 2 wings, 2 drumsticks, 2 bone thighs and 2 breasts. All the trimmings go to the stock pot.

GURKHA CURRY

As with all cooking, this recipe is best when the freshest ingredients are used. However, do not hesitate to make it with dried spices and canned tomatoes. However you make it, it's a wonderful aromatic spicy dish that is a welcome dish outdoors.

INGREDIENTS

Serves 4

about 500g (1lb) skinless boneless chicken thighs or any other available meat
1 medium onion
2 garlic cloves
2.5cm (1in) piece of fresh root ginger
1 fresh green chilli, seeded and finely chopped, or ¼ tsp chilli powder
4 tbsp vegetable oil
½ cinnamon stick
4 cloves
4 cardamom pods
½ tsp ground turmeric
1 tbsp garam masala (more if you like it spicy)
4 tomatoes, chopped, or 1 x 400g (15oz) can of chopped tomatoes
pinch of sugar, if using canned tomatoes
2 tbsp tomato puree
water, if necessary
salt and ground black pepper, to taste
Plain White Rice (see page 181), to serve

METHOD

1 Cut the chicken or meat into bite-sized pieces. Peel and chop the onion, peel and crush the garlic and peel and grate the ginger. Seed and finely chop the chilli.

2 Gently heat the oil in a cast-iron pan with the cinnamon stick, cloves and cardamom pods.

3 When a nice aroma rises from the spices, add the chicken or meat. Cook until well browned.

4 Add the chopped onion and fry for about 15 minutes, until soft and golden.

5 Add the garlic, ginger, turmeric, garam masala and chopped chilli or chilli powder. Stir all the time to prevent any burning.

6 Now add the chopped tomatoes, sugar, if using, and tomato puree. If you feel you need to, add a splash of water.

7 Cover the pan and simmer for 10–15 minutes, then taste and season the curry. You may need to add a little more sugar if using canned tomatoes.

8 Turn off the heat and let the curry rest for 5 minutes. Check the chicken or meat is cooked through before serving with Plain White Rice.

VARIATION

For a vegetarian version, simply swap the chicken or meat for vegetables, such as aubergines, potatoes, courgettes, peppers or whatever you have to hand, peeled or seeded if necessary and cut into bite-sized pieces.

ALOO CHAAT - INDIAN FRIED POTATOES

This is a classic food of the street market – what better recommendation do you need? It is delicious and really easy to cook outdoors. It is a wonderful accompaniment to Gurkha curry.

INGREDIENTS

Serves 4

4 medium potatoes
1 medium onion
1 small fresh green chilli
2 tbsp oil
4 tbsp tomato puree
½ cup (125ml) water
pinch of salt
2 tsp chilli flakes
2 tsp ground coriander
2 tsp *chaat masala* (see box)
juice of ½ lemon
fresh coriander leaves, chopped, to garnish

METHOD

1 Boil the potatoes, whole and in their skins, for about 15 minutes, or until cooked. Drain, leave to cool slightly, then peel and cut into bite-sized pieces.
2 Peel and finely chop the onion, and deseed and chop the green chilli medium fine.
3 Heat the oil in a cast-iron pan and sweat down the onion for about 15 minutes, until translucent, adding the chilli about 10 minutes into the cooking time.

4 Add the tomato puree and the water, then add some salt, chilli flakes, ground coriander and *chaat masala*. Stir well and reduce the mixture to a paste.
5 Add the potatoes to the mixture and carefully turn until well coated.
6 Remove from the heat, squeeze over the lemon juice and serve garnished with freshly chopped coriander leaves.

CHAAT MASALA

INGREDIENTS:
3 tbsp ground cumin
2 tbsp ground coriander
4 tbsp amchoor (green mango powder)
1½ tsp ground ginger
2 tbsp powdered black salt
1½ tsp ground black pepper
¼ tsp asafoetida
1 tsp chilli powder
1 tsp powdered mint
1½ tsp ajwain (carom powder)

Chaat masala can easily be purchased ready made, but if you would like to make your own, it is very easy. The best way is to use fresh seeds, to liberate the aromas in a hot pan and then to grind them yourself, which is wonderful if the time and facilities are available. Failing that, do as I do and mix the powders listed opposite. Make plenty and store it in a light and airtight jar. Just a small amount of this wonderful spice mix sprinkled on vegetarian dishes at the completion of cooking will elevate them. It is also good on green salads, sliced tomatoes and cucumbers. You may be surprised how often you use this mix. But do not confuse with garam masala: they are quite different.

KAENG PA - THAI JUNGLE CURRY

A classic dish from Northern Thailand, *kaeng pa* is characterised by the absence of coconut milk, which reflects the unavailability of coconuts far from the coast. Although this has become a popular restaurant dish, to appreciate it at its best it has to be eaten in the jungle, where its versatility becomes abundantly clear.

The red curry paste is usually carried wrapped in a piece of plastic and perhaps some fish sauce is packed in an old drinks bottle, alongside some oil. The pan is hastily propped between three stones and heated with split bamboo. In goes the oil, more than we would use at home, and then the red curry paste, which contains so many chillies that molten lava would cool the mouth. Then in goes the protein, whatever is available – river shrimp, catfish, wild boar, venison, all manner of birds, frogs or even snails. The sauce is now thinned with water and the vegetables are added: hearts of palm, bamboo shoots or any edible vegetables the jungle can provide. It is usually served with sticky rice steamed in a bamboo tube (see page 65). Split open the bamboo tube with a *parang* (machete), whereupon one half holds the rice and the other half the curry.

Eating this delicious dish, one breaks out in a sweat that makes the stifling tropical humidity seem chilly. My recipe is less spicy by far. I have found it just as versatile outside of the jungle – brilliant in a hunting or fishing camp, for example.

INGREDIENTS

Serves 4

500g (1lb) pork
8 baby corn
small handful of green beans
4 Thai aubergines or 1 European aubergine
2 *krachai* (finger roots) or 2.5cm (1in) piece of fresh root ginger
1 fresh red chilli
4 kaffir lime leaves or the grated rind of 3 limes
2 tbsp oil
2 tbsp Thai red curry paste
about 2 cups (500ml) water or chicken stock (see page 261)
2 tbsp fish sauce
Sticky Rice in a Pan (see page 183) or jasmine rice, to serve

METHOD

1 Slice the pork, baby corn and green beans into bite-sized pieces.
2 Remove the stems and wash and quarter the Thai aubergines, or dice a European aubergine into bite-sized pieces.
3 Peel and finely slice the finger roots or ginger lengthways into fine matchsticks, then seed the chilli and slice into fine matchsticks too. Finely slice the lime leaves if using.
4 Heat the oil in a cast-iron pan over a gentle heat, then add the curry paste and cook until the aromas are rising nicely.
5 Add the pork and cook quickly until half cooked. Add the water or stock, sufficient to just cover the meat. Add the fish sauce and the vegetables.
6 Bring to a low simmer and cook for about 20 minutes, or until the meat is tender.
7 Serve with Sticky Rice in a Pan or jasmine rice.

RENDANG CURRY

This slow-cooked curry, commonly dubbed the 'King of Curries', is a wonder of flavour. It is usually made with cheaper, tougher cuts of meat, which break down during the slow cooking and absorb all the wonderful spices. I like to honour the recipe with best venison or beef braising steak, however, which results in a shorter cooking time, but you can use any meat, red types being the best. If using other cuts, allow a longer cooking time. Some people prefer to remove the harder spices, but I like to leave them in – it's entirely up to you.

INGREDIENTS

Serves 4

500g (1lb) best braising venison or beef steak
Malaysian curry powder for meat (check the quantity required on the packet; beware, these can be explosively hot!)
5 shallots or 1 medium onion
5cm (2in) piece of fresh root ginger
3 lemongrass stems
3 tbsp oil
1 cinnamon stick
4 star anise
pinch of salt
1¼ cups (120g) desiccated coconut
water
1 tbsp palm sugar or honey
Coconut Rice (see page 183), to serve

METHOD

1 Coat each piece of meat in curry powder and leave to marinate for an hour.

2 Peel and chop the shallots or onion, and peel and roughly slice the ginger and the lemongrass.

3 Heat the oil in a cast-iron pan over a moderate heat, then add the spices and when their aromas rise from the pan, add the onion or shallots and fry for about 15 minutes, until translucent.

4 Add the meat and keep it moving as it browns. Once brown, add the salt, along with the ginger and lemongrass, and cook for 2 minutes.

5 Raise the pot to reduce the heat and cook slowly until the curry is nearly dry (about 30 minutes), then add sufficient water to prevent the curry from burning, but not enough to come level with the top of the meat.

6 Put the lid on and allow to cook slowly for 1 hour. Do not allow the curry to dry out. Check frequently, stirring the curry each time.

7 Meanwhile, prepare the *kerisek* by dry frying the desiccated coconut until it is golden. Be sure to keep an eye on it to prevent it from burning.

8 Once the curry has reduced to your preferred consistency, taste and season if required with extra salt and some palm sugar or honey, to taste.

9 Add the *kerisek*, mixing in well. Simmer at the lowest heat for 10 minutes. If using an iron camp oven, simply remove it from the heat.

10 Meanwhile, prepare the Coconut Rice, then serve.

BEER BREAD

This is a classic recipe from the Australian Outback. I long ago lost count of the number of these loaves that I have baked over the years. It is very quick and easy to bake, tastes wonderful and is always popular, especially with butter, golden syrup and a mug of billy tea.

INGREDIENTS

Makes 1 loaf

2 cups (250g) plain flour, plus extra for dusting
2 tsp baking powder
½ tsp salt
about ⅔ cup (175ml) beer

METHOD

1 Mix the dry ingredients well and then add the beer a little at a time until the dough is holding together well. The beer provides a yeast bread-like flavour.
2 Sprinkle some flour in the base of a preheated camp oven – a layer 2–3mm in depth will do.
3 Place the loaf in the oven and with a sharp knife, slash a cross in the top of it.
4 Put the lid on and cook the bread surrounded by embers. Finish the beer that is left over. Check the bread after 30–40 minutes.
5 Once the loaf appears to be reaching completion, place embers on top of the lid to brown the crust.
6 Test the bread with a skewer. When it can be drawn out dry, remove the pan from the heat, turn out the loaf and allow it to rest prior to serving, though few have the patience to let it cool for long.

NO-NEED BREAD

Jim Lahey, founder of the Sullivan Street Bakery in Hell's Kitchen, Manhattan, New York came up with this brilliant recipe. I call it 'No-Need Bread' because for all practical purposes, there is no need for any other recipe in a field kitchen. I like to make the dough late in the afternoon and to leave it to rise overnight in a protected place, such as a storage box or tent vestibule. In cold weather, the bowl can be insulated from the cold ground by placing it on two pieces of firewood and wrapping it in a spare coat. This bread is a firm favourite in a fixed camp.

INGREDIENTS

Makes 1 loaf

3 cups (375g) strong white bread flour, plus extra for dusting
½ tsp fast-action dried yeast
1½ tsp salt
1⅓ cups (330ml) water

METHOD

1 Mix the dry ingredients together well, then add the water and quickly mix through.

2 Cover the mixing bowl and leave overnight, ideally for 12 hours.

3 Transfer the dough to a lightly floured surface. Flatten it down slightly, then fold in the left and right sides, then the top and bottom sides.

4 Flour a clean dish towel or large bandana, then place the dough on top of it, folded side down. Flour the top of the loaf and fold over the cloth.

5 Leave in a warm place while you prepare a camp oven and heat it until it is very hot. I find placing the inverted mixing bowl over the wrapped loaf gives sufficient protection from the elements.

6 Take the dough, turn it over and place it in the oven.

7 Place the oven with embers surrounding it and bake the bread for 30 minutes.

8 Lift the lid for 2 minutes and inspect the bread. Replace the lid and put embers on top to finish off the cooking and to brown the crust – roughly 10 minutes. By all means lift the lid to check on the cooking during this time.

9 Remove the bread from the oven and leave to cool slightly before you attempt to slice it.

WHOLEMEAL LOAF

For a wholemeal version, use the ingredients below and increase the cooking time by 5–10 minutes.

INGREDIENTS:
2 cups (250g) rye or wholemeal bread flour
1 cup (125g) strong white bread flour, plus extra for dusting
½ tsp fast-action dried yeast
1½ tsp salt
1½ cups (375ml) water

NO-NEED-TO-WAIT BREAD

If I need to make my loaf more quickly, I use the same recipe as for No-Need Bread, but using warm water and with the addition of ¼ tsp ascorbic acid (vitamin C). This speeds up the rising time and increases the dough's volume. If you have none to hand, just use very warm water (50°C/122°F) or an extra ½ tsp yeast.

INGREDIENTS

Makes 1 loaf

3 cups (375g) strong white bread flour, plus extra for dusting
½ tsp fast-action dried yeast
¼ tsp salt
½ tsp ascorbic acid
1½ cups (375ml) warm water

METHOD

1 Mix the dry ingredients well, then add the water and quickly mix through.

2 Cover the bowl, then wrap it in a spare jacket or pullover for insulation and leave to rise for 3–6 hours. In cold weather, I place the mixing bowl floating in warm (not hot) water contained in a second bowl and cover both with a spare jersey or coat. This creates a perfect proving environment that can cope with the vagaries of the outdoor kitchen.

3 Turn the dough out onto a lightly floured surface, flatten down slightly, then fold in the left and right sides, then the top and bottom sides.

4 Flour a clean dish towel or large bandana, then place the dough on top of it, folded side down. Flour the top of the loaf and fold over the cloth.

5 Leave in a warm place while you prepare a camp oven and heat until it is very hot. I find placing the inverted mixing bowl over the wrapped loaf gives sufficient protection from the elements.

6 Take the dough, turn it over and place it in the oven.

7 Place the oven with embers surrounding it and bake the bread for 30 minutes.

8 Lift the lid for 2 minutes and inspect the bread. Replace the lid and put embers on top to finish the cooking and to brown the crust – roughly 10 minutes. By all means, lift the lid to check on the cooking during this time.

9 Remove the bread from the oven and leave to cool slightly before you attempt to slice it.

THE ADVANTAGE OF THE NO-KNEAD BREADS

Travelling in remote places requires energy and application so the thought of kneading a loaf is no hardship. Actually, kneading bread is a great way to generate warmth on a cold day. The benefit of these recipes outdoors therefore does not lie in the lack of kneading, but in the fact that a surface to knead on is not essential. With some care, these doughs can be made totally in a mixing bowl or finished on a clean bandana spread out on a sleeping mat.

CAMP OVEN WHITE LOAF

This loaf takes a little more time and effort than no-need-to-wait bread, but results in a loaf with a tighter crumb. Once you master the kneading, it is a really satisfying bread to make. Given the requirement for a second rising I reserve this recipe for warm weather or cooking in cabins.

INGREDIENTS

Makes 1 loaf

4 cups (500g) strong white bread flour, plus extra for dusting

2½ tsp fast-action dried yeast

2 tbsp butter, softened by the fire, or olive oil

2 cups (500ml) cold water

1½ tsp salt

METHOD

1 In a mixing bowl, combine the flour and the yeast and mix well.

2 Rub in the softened butter or olive oil, then add a cup of water and mix well, to begin forming a dough. Add the salt and more water, a little at a time, until a soft, dry dough forms. The dough should clean the inside of the mixing bowl.

3 Lightly flour a work surface and knead the dough until it reaches that magical stage when it is elastic and smooth. As a guide, this will take about 10 minutes.

4 Return the dough to the mixing bowl, cover with a cloth and allow to rise until doubled in size, usually around 2 hours, in a protected place – inside a tent or vehicle is perfect.

5 Transfer the dough to a lightly floured surface, then flatten slightly and fold in the edges. Turn the dough over and with the edge of your hand, round it into a ball using the bottom edge of your hand to tuck the dough under with each turn.

6 Invert the mixing bowl over the dough and leave to prove for about an hour. During this time, prepare the fire and heat a camp oven. Sprinkle a 2–3mm-thick layer of flour onto the base of the camp oven.

7 Remove the mixing bowl. The dough should have doubled in size. Slash a diamond or other pattern into the skin of the dough to allow it to rise evenly.

8 Drop the dough into the camp oven, replace the lid and surround with embers. Bake for 25–30 minutes, then check the loaf. Finish colouring the crust by placing some embers on the lid and baking for a further 5–10 minutes.

9 Remove the loaf from the oven and leave to cool slightly before slicing and eating.

BREAD ROLLS

Once you have mastered baking the previous bread, have a go at making your own bread rolls. The still connected rolls are an impressive reveal from a camp oven and there is no better addition to a freshly made soup.

INGREDIENTS

Makes 7 rolls

1¼ tsp rapid-rise dried yeast

2 cups (250g) strong white bread flour, plus extra for dusting

1 tbsp butter, softened by the fire

1 tsp salt

1½ cups (375ml) water

olive oil

METHOD

1 Mix the yeast with the flour, then blend in the softened butter and the salt.

2 Add the water and form into a dough.

3 Turn out onto a lightly floured surface and knead the dough for 10 minutes or until it is elastic with a smooth skin.

4 Place in a lightly oiled bowl, cover with a cloth and set aside to rise for 1–2 hours, until doubled in size.

5 Turn the dough out onto a lightly floured surface and flatten slightly, folding the top and bottom into the centre, followed by the left and right edges.

6 Roll the dough into a cylinder shape and slice into seven equal segments. Roll each segment into a ball.

7 Place one ball in the centre of your camp oven with the remaining six placed equally spaced around it but not touching. Put the lid on the oven and set aside in a protected place until the dough has once again doubled in size. During this time, prepare the fire.

8 Take the oven to the fire and bury it in embers. Bake the bread rolls for 30 minutes, or until they are golden and sound hollow when tapped on their undersides.

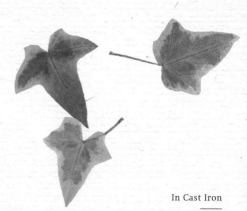

CAMP OVEN SPELT LOAF

Spelt flour contains less gluten than conventional bread flour, more fibre, is rich in fatty acids, amino acids and vitamins E and B2. It's little wonder that many eat this bread for its medicinal value. For me though it is the allure of a spelt loafs rustic charm, its delightful nutty, almost earthy, flavour.

INGREDIENTS

Makes 1 loaf

2 cups (500ml) warm water

1 tsp fast-action dried yeast

1 tbsp honey (optional)

3 cups (375g) spelt flour, plus extra for dusting

1 tsp salt

2 tbsp oil

METHOD

1 Mix the water with the yeast and honey, if using. I use warm water for this.

2 In a mixing bowl, combine the flour, salt and oil and mix. Add the yeast liquid and mix well.

3 Cover the bowl with a clean cloth and leave in a sheltered place to rise overnight.

4 Transfer the dough to a lightly floured surface. Flatten slightly and fold in the edges. Turn the dough over and with the edge of your hand, round it into a ball using the bottom edge of your hand to tuck the dough under with each turn.

5 Invert the mixing bowl over the dough and leave to prove for about an hour.

6 During this time, prepare the fire and heat a camp oven. Sprinkle a 2–3mm-thick layer of flour onto the base of the camp oven.

7 Remove the mixing bowl. The dough should have doubled in size. Slash a diamond or other pattern into the skin of the dough to allow it to rise evenly.

8 Drop the dough into the camp oven, replace the lid and surround with embers. Bake for 25–30 minutes, then check the loaf. Finish colouring the crust by placing some embers on the lid and bake for a further 5–10 minutes.

9 Remove the loaf from the oven and leave to cool slightly before slicing and eating.

In Cast Iron

PIZZA

Pizza needs no introduction, what always surprises me is how readily we reach for premade pizza bases when it is so easy to make a delicious, fresh pizza dough. Making pizzas in a fixed camp is great fun and all ages love to experiment with their own toppings.

INGREDIENTS

1 cup (250ml) lukewarm water
1 tsp rapid-rise dried yeast
1 tsp sugar
3 cups (375g) strong white bread flour, plus extra for dusting
1 tsp salt
1 tbsp olive oil
tomato puree or passata

METHOD

1 Blend the water, yeast and sugar in a small bowl.

2 Place the flour in a mixing bowl and add the salt. Mix well. Add the oil and stir into the flour, then add the yeast mixture and mix well with your fingertips.

3 Knead the dough in the mixing bowl or preferably on a lightly floured board for about 10 minutes, until it is elastic with a smooth skin.

4 Set aside in the mixing bowl covered lightly with a cloth in a protected place for 1–2 hours, until it has doubled in size.

5 Preheat your camp oven.

6 Cut the dough into sections of a size appropriate for your pan. Roll into balls.

7 Take a ball of dough, flatten it and gradually work it out into a wide, flat disc. Traditionally this is done in the hand but if you lack this skill, stretch it out by pressing, pinching and pulling it to the desired size.

8 Leaving the edge of the dough disc clear, top the pizza first with tomato puree or passata and then the toppings of your choice.

9 If you have a Petromax Dutch Oven or similar, the pizza can be cooked directly on the underside of the oven lid with the base inverted over the top as a lid. Otherwise, cook directly in the camp oven or on a plate raised in the oven on three stones. I prefer to cook directly on the base.

10 Cook the pizza for 10-20 minutes before checking (to avoid letting the heat out of the oven and reducing the temperature).

11 Extract the pizza from the oven with a fish slice and cook the remainder in the same way.

TOPPING CREATIVITY

Obviously, what you top your pizza with will depend upon what you have, and what you like. It is fun to be creative, but the golden rule is DO NOT overload the pizza, as it may become soggy and the toppings may not cook properly.

STINGING NETTLE QUICHE

Quiche is fabulously adaptable, a great meal served with a salad – particularly a salad containing some slightly bitter wild salad leaves. Other flavourings for the quiche could include thyme, pancetta, bacon, tomato, basil, broccoli, wild mushrooms, caramelised onion, prawns, mozzarella, Brie or goat's cheese... There is almost no limit to what can be incorporated.

INGREDIENTS

Serves 4–6

For the pastry
2 cups (250g) plain flour, plus extra for dusting
½ tsp salt
½ cup (125g) butter
3–4 tbsp cold water
beaten egg or 2 tsp powdered egg mixed with 4 tsp cold water

For the filling
1 cup fresh stinging nettle tops
1 cup (125g) grated Cheddar cheese
8 tbsp powdered egg
½ tsp salt
1½ cups (375ml) evaporated milk or 9 tbsp milk powder and 1½ cups (375ml) warm water

METHOD

1 For the pastry, aerate the flour by shaking it into a large bowl, then whisk in the salt.

2 Dice the butter and delicately rub it into the flour until you have a crumb texture. Add water a teaspoon at a time, until the pastry is just holding together.

3 Knead the pastry very briefly until smooth. Do not overwork or it will be rubbery and tough. Set aside in a covered bowl in a cool spot to rest (see page 242).

4 Preheat your camp oven.

5 On a well-floured surface with a well-floured rolling pin, roll the pastry dough out into a circle or rectangle to fit your tin or receptacle. This could be a suitable baking tray or even a deep billycan lid.

6 Line your chosen vessel with the pastry, brush with egg or the egg mixture, then prick lightly all over with a fork and weight it down with uncooked rice.

7 Blind bake the pastry case (see page 47) for about 15 minutes, until light golden.

8 Meanwhile, make the filling. To a billycan half-filled with boiling water, add a cup full of fresh nettle tops. After 1 minute, strain really well, squashing out as much liquid from the nettles as possible. Put the nettles in a clean cloth and squeeze them. If they are too wet, they'll make the quiche soggy. Roughly chop the dried nettles (they will now have lost their stings).

9 Spread grated cheese across the base of the quiche and arrange the nettle tops atop that.

10 Whisk the powdered egg and salt into the evaporated milk. If using milk powder, combine the egg, salt and milk powder and reconstitute by whisking in warm water to the consistency of a single cream.

11 Pour the mixture into the quiche base over the filling.

12 Bake the quiche in the camp oven for 30–40 minutes, until a skewer inserted in the middle comes out clean.

APPLE PIE

Apple Pie, do I really need to say more? Pie making is easy outdoors with a camp oven, you can experiment with all manner of savoury and sweet fillings but your journey in the world of pies will always cycle back to the humbly delightful apple pie.

INGREDIENTS

Serves 4–6

For the pastry
2 cups (250g) plain
  flour, plus extra
  for dusting
½ tsp salt
½ tsp sugar
½ cup (125g) butter
3–4 tbsp cold water
2 tsp powdered egg
  and 2 tsp water, for
  the glaze

For the filling
6–8 Granny Smith
  apples or equivalent
  (in the tropics, use
  green mangoes)
½ cup (100g) brown
  sugar
2 tbsp plain flour
2 tbsp lemon juice
¼ tsp grated nutmeg
¼ tsp ground ginger

METHOD

1 For the pastry, aerate the flour by shaking it into a large bowl, then whisk in the salt and the sugar.
2 Dice the butter and delicately rub it into the flour until you have a crumb texture. Add water a teaspoon at a time until the pastry is just holding together.
3 Knead the pastry very briefly until smooth. Do not overwork or it will become rubbery and tough. Set aside in a covered bowl in a cool spot to rest. See the box below for what to do in other conditions.
4 Preheat a camp oven.
5 Roll the pastry dough out into a circle to fit on top of your pie dish on a well-floured surface with a well-floured rolling pin.
6 For the filling, peel and finely slice the apples, then add the brown sugar, flour, lemon juice, nutmeg and ground ginger. Mix well and arrange in a pie dish.
7 Place the pastry on top and crimp down the edge. Mix the powdered egg and water for the glaze and brush over the pastry surface. Pierce the pastry top in several places with a knife tip to allow steam to escape during the baking process.
8 Bake for 50–60 minutes in the camp oven until the pastry is crisp and golden brown. Allow to cool slightly before serving.

MAKING PASTRY IN DIFFERENT CONDITIONS

If the weather is warm, make the pastry dough the night before, then leave to rest and chill overnight. In very hot conditions, cover the dough with a metal billycan or mixing bowl and drape a wet cloth over the vessel so that it is cooled by the process of evaporation. Wake early and complete the quiche in the cool of the dawn.

CRUMBLE

Crumble is very quick and easy to cook outdoors, with no pastry or rising issues to contend with. It's also incredibly versatile, not to mention tasty. What's not to love?

INGREDIENTS

Serves 4–6

For the crumble topping
1½ cups (200g) plain flour (for Rhubarb Crumble, use 50:50 plain flour and ground almonds)
⅓ cup (75g) butter
⅓ cup (65g) brown sugar

For the filling
See method

METHOD

1 For the crumble topping, put the flour in a bowl, dice the butter and with your fingertips, rub it in with the flour until you have a crumb texture.
2 Add the sugar and continue until it is also combined.

For Rhubarb Crumble

3 For this, canned rhubarb can be used for convenience. In which case just put it in a suitable dish, such as a billycan or lid, and perhaps taste and adjust the sweetness. Add some ground cinnamon if liked and if you have it.
4 For fresh rhubarb, trim a few stalks of rhubarb and cut into chunks, then combine with a few spoonfuls of sugar and sweat in a billycan for 15 minutes over a low heat. The amount of sugar you need will vary, so go by taste. Use a spoon to push the chunks down and ensure even cooking. Do not overcook the rhubarb; it should remain chunky. You may need to spoon off some surplus juice if the mixture seems too liquid, or else stir through a few spoonfuls of ground almonds, which will soak up some of the liquid and thicken it. Transfer to your chosen dish.
5 Cover with the crumble topping, pat down firmly and bake in a preheated camp oven for 30 minutes.

**For Wild Blackberry Crumble
or Wild Raspberry Crumble**

3 Put the fruit in the cooking pan – billycan or lid – and sprinkle a little sugar over the top.
4 Cover with the crumble topping, pat down firmly and bake for 30 minutes in a preheated camp oven until the crumble is golden.

VARIATION

You could substitute half of the plain flour in the crumble mixture with quick-cook rolled oats for a nubbly texture and nutty flavour.

QUICK CAKE RECIPE

This basic cake mix is really easy to make and bake, and produces a delicious light sponge. It is very versatile, so I've provided lots of flavour variations and additions. Or, experiment with what you have to hand; so long as the basic mix is correct and the additions aren't too wet, it will be fine.

INGREDIENTS

Makes 1

1 cup (125g) self-raising flour, plus extra for dusting
1 tsp baking powder
4 tbsp powdered egg or 2 eggs
4 tbsp water, if using powdered egg
½ cup (125g) margarine or butter
2 tbsp of sugar

METHOD

1 Prepare a camp oven and grease and flour a 20cm (8in) cake tin.
2 Aerate the flour by shaking it into a bowl, then stir in the baking powder and powdered egg, if using. Combine with the water, if using powdered egg, then add the margarine or butter and sugar. If you have fresh eggs, omit the powdered egg and water and add the eggs with the margarine and sugar.
3 Mix together until smooth and glossy, then scrape into the prepared tin and smooth the top level.

4 Bake in the preheated camp oven for 25 minutes.
5 Test the cake: when a skewer is inserted and can be withdrawn dry, it is done. Alternatively, use an instant-read thermometer; when it reads 95–98°C in the cake centre, it is ready.
6 Remove from the tin and leave to cool.

CHOCOLATE CAKE

INGREDIENTS:
3 tbsp cocoa powder or grated 100% cocoa drinking chocolate
3 tbsp boiling water

METHOD: Dissolve the cocoa or chocolate in the water and combine with the cake mixture in Step 2.

COFFEE AND WALNUT CAKE

INGREDIENTS:
2 tsp instant coffee
1 tsp boiling water
½ cup (50g) chopped walnuts

METHOD: Dissolve the instant coffee in the boiling water and add to the cake mixture in Step 2. Fold the walnuts through the cake mixture in Step 3.

CITRUS CAKE

INGREDIENTS:
juice of 2 lemons or limes, or 1 orange
2 tsp grated lemon, orange or lime rind
2 tbsp sugar

METHOD: Add 2 tsp of the juice and the rind to the cake mixture in Step 2. Dissolve the sugar in the remaining juice, pierce holes into the crust with a skewer and drizzle the juice over the top.

BANANA LOAF

I consider banana loaf to be an essential outdoor recipe, being tasty, sustaining and comforting. It is always good to have fresh fruit in the camp, not least bananas. In the tropics, I try to purchase whole branches; sometimes the little sweet bananas are available.

INGREDIENTS

Makes 1 loaf

4 ripe medium bananas
1 cup (250g) sugar
½ cup (125g) butter, plus extra for greasing
2 cups (250g) plain flour
4 tbsp powdered egg, plus 12 tbsp water or 2 eggs
2 tsp baking powder

METHOD

1 Prepare a camp oven and grease a billycan lid or a bread tin.
2 With a fork, mash the bananas and the sugar together until really smooth and creamy.
3 Soften the butter and work it into the mixture. Stir in the real eggs, if using.
4 Aerate the flour and stir in the powdered egg and water, if using, and the baking powder. Add the dry mixture to the wet and gently fold together.
5 Pour the cake mixture into a greased billycan lid or a bread tin and smooth the top level.

6 Bake in a camp oven for 40 minutes until when tested by piercing with a skewer, the skewer emerges dry or the temperature in the loaf's centre is 95–98°C when probed with an instant-read thermometer.
7 Remove from the tin and leave to cool.

CHOCOLATE CHIP COOKIES

Cookies are always popular outdoors, especially when engaged in strenuous pursuits or coping with challenging weather. Every wilderness chef should have some cookie recipes up their sleeve. A plate of still-warm cookies with a pot of fresh coffee is a wonderful boost to morale.

INGREDIENTS

Makes about 12 cookies

⅓ cup (75g) butter, plus extra for greasing
3 tbsp brown sugar
4 tbsp powdered hot chocolate (standard chocolate powder, not grated chocolate)
1 cup (125g) plain flour
½ tsp baking powder
2 tbsp powdered egg, plus 6 tbsp water

METHOD

1 Preheat a reflector or camp oven and grease a baking tray.
2 In a small billycan, melt the butter and the sugar, then stir in the powdered chocolate. Remove from the heat and allow to cool.
3 Aerate the flour and stir in the baking powder and the powdered egg.
4 Little by little, stir the dry mix into the butter and sugar until well combined.
5 Take 1 tbsp at a time and form into balls. Place these on the prepared baking tray, allowing plenty of room between each one for the mixture to spread.
6 Bake in a reflector oven or camp oven for 10 minutes.
7 Remove from the heat, transfer to a plate or chopping board and leave to cool.

VARIATION

For double chocolate chip cookies, stir in a handful of chocolate chips or chopped chocolate when you add the dry ingredients.

FRUIT AND NUT OAT BAR

This simple fruit and nut bar is great trail food. Make it before hiking from your base camp to a fly camp. Use your imagination to modify the recipe and add wild fruit you have foraged and dried yourself.

INGREDIENTS

Makes 6–8 bars

butter, for greasing
2 bananas
1 tbsp honey or maple
  syrup
1 cup (75g) quick-cook
  rolled oats
2 tbsp currants or
  mixed dried fruit
2 tbsp hazelnuts

METHOD

1 Preheat a camp or reflector oven and grease a plate.
2 Mash the bananas into a smooth cream, then stir in the honey or maple syrup. Mix in the oats and the currants or mixed dried fruit.
3 Chop the hazelnuts into small pieces and add them to the mix.
4 The mixture can be patted out on the buttered plate to a 1–2cm (½–1in) thickness or rolled into walnut-sized balls and then flattened and placed on the plate.

5 Bake in a dutch oven or reflector oven until golden. Remove from the heat and allow to cool.
6 If baked as one large piece, it can subsequently be sliced with a knife to convenient portions.

GROUND OVEN

'THE INDIANS PREPARED A LARGE FIRE OF DRIED WOOD, on which was thrown a number of smooth stones from the river. As soon as the fire went down and the stones were heated they were laid next to each other in a level position and covered with a quantity of branches of pine, on which were placed bear flesh, the boughs and the flesh alternated for several courses, leaving a thick layer of pine on the top. On this heap was then placed a small quantity of water, and the whole covered with earth to the depth of 4 inches. After remaining in this state about three hours the meat was taken off.' ELLIOT COUES, 1893*

I have been making ground ovens for over 40 years now and the joy of this cooking method has never faded. Despite the simplicity of the concept, there is a wonder in it that touches a deep vestigial memory. Every time the scent of well-cooked ingredients rises from the pit, it is like watching a magician pull a rabbit from his hat.

But do not be fooled: for all its simplicity, to make a ground oven work there are technical requirements that must be met. I have several times seen ground ovens fail on survival courses when the instructor did not fully appreciate the finer points of the process.

USAGE PAST AND PRESENT

Ground ovens have been used for thousands of years. The earliest evidence so far dates to around 29,000 years at the Pavlov VI archaeological site in the south-east of the Czech Republic, where hunter-gatherers were cooking mammoth. However, I'm certain that the use of ground ovens predates this and merely left no trace; the simplest ground ovens are shallow and easily destroyed by natural degradation and human activities such as ploughing.

---

* Hough, W., *Fire as an Agent in Human Culture* (Forgotten Books, 2017)

When they are located, ground ovens rarely tell us much about why they were used or what was being cooked within them. An exception to this is the tantalising site at Staosnaig, on the island of Colonsay, Scotland. In the early 1990s, excavations here revealed Mesolithic ground ovens that contained remains of hazelnuts along with some apple cores and lesser celandine roots.* One of these ovens had overcooked and been abandoned, providing a precious insight to ancient cooking. As a result, we now know for sure that this shallow oven had been used to cook a mass of hazelnuts. Working with my friend and colleague, the late Professor Gordon Hillman, I duly experimented with this method and discovered that hazelnuts cooked in this way become a delicious staple food and can be easily preserved.

Proving their usefulness, ground ovens are still widely used today, surviving both as a practical means of food processing and a focus of cultural feasting. In Australia, for example, I have many times witnessed ground ovens being used to bulk process edible yams, both as a stage in the processing of toxic roots and simply to impart a good flavour to barramundi fish. Interestingly, Australian aboriginal communities still preserve a detailed understanding of these original cooking methods, using embers to cook certain foods and ground ovens for others, as specified in their cultural law. In New Zealand, meanwhile, a large ground oven called a *hangi* is used to cook a wide range of food types and is often the focus for the whole community. While it is cooking, families chat and laugh together, anchored by the forthcoming meal. When the oven is opened, the food is served in the community hall.

In Samoa, the *umu* is made by heating a pile of volcanic rocks. The food is wrapped in leaves or placed in baskets that are laid upon the heated rocks and then covered with a series of mats to trap the heat. I have only to close my eyes to recall the wonderful, delicately smoky flavour of yam cooked in this way. In the Torres Strait, too, ground ovens are in widespread use, cooking all manner of seafood. From these experiences and many others, I have learned much about the diversity of ground ovens and it has been a mind-broadening experience.

WHY GROUND OVENS?

The most obvious benefit of using a ground oven is the ease with which many people can be fed without the need for a cooking utensil. In Polynesia, for instance, ground ovens are frequently used to feed parties at social celebrations. This continues in line with ancient tradition, as testified by a pit oven, estimated to be 9,000 years old, that was discovered in Western Cyprus and is believed to have been used to cater for up to 200 diners.

But more than just being an economical way of cooking, ground ovens offer other important benefits. Globally, they are widely employed in the cooking of plant foods, the long steaming process providing a higher caloric return than cooking plants directly in the embers. Ground ovens also allow prolonged cooking. For example, the Apache would cook agave hearts for four days. This long steaming

---

* Mithen, S., *After the Ice* (Weidenfeld & Nicolson, 2011)

can also be used to denature or modify plant toxins, the classic example being the cheeky yam of northern Australia. These toxic yams are steamed in a ground oven before being grated using a snail shell grater and then washed in a stream in a special dilly bag (basket) to remove their toxins. The steaming is a vital step in the processing, and while it is a lot of work, it's worth the effort; modern analysis has shown that the processed cheeky yam is 30–40% richer in carbohydrate than the more edible long yam that is also gathered in the same region and is cooked in a different way.

Fish are also frequently cooked in ground ovens, usually larger fish species and the larger shellfish. This reduces the risk of overcooking the fish, but also allows many fish to be cooked simultaneously. What's more, they can easily be flavoured with herbs and aromatic plants. In both Australia and the Pacific Coast regions of Canada, I have encountered families with their own recipes for flavourful ground oven-cooked dishes. This flavouring of food is an important benefit that is frequently forgotten by researchers.

Ground ovens also provide a useful way to cook meat, particularly large joints. I have never seen a mammoth leg cooked underground,

but I still chuckle at the memory of pulling an emu leg out of a ground oven cooked by a Pitjantjatjara elder – quite literally a drumstick fit for a giant! Once again, it is hard to overcook the food and there are added nutritional benefits from cooking food in this manner. What's more, there is also a very significant saving in the amount of fuel required when compared to cooking on an open fire. Interestingly, the Pitjantjatjara ground oven was made conveniently close to the kill site to cook the leg immediately, the remainder of the carcass being taken back to the village for later consumption.

In village sites, it is not uncommon for a ground oven to be used for many years, even generations. Inevitably, this results in a pile of fire-broken rocks built up to one side of the oven, along with a midden mound of food remains. Both are traces that survive well in the archaeological record. But ground ovens are also used in an impromptu way for immediate use away from places of settlement. These simple, shallow ground ovens of immediacy interest me as they are all but invisible in the archaeological record but incredibly practical in the field.

HOW TO BUILD A SIMPLE GROUND OVEN

Any ground oven is built to suit the shape and/or quantity of food to be cooked within it. The shape must be optimised to minimise effort. For plant foods and shellfish, small fish or meat, the oven is usually built in a round shape. For larger game, a more oval-shaped oven better accommodates the food. Communal ovens are usually rectangular. An oven intended for long-term use is best lined with slabs of rock, as are ovens made in damper or colder soil and those used predominantly for dry cooking.

THE GROUND AND THE PIT

For the best result, dig the oven pit in dry ground; damp ground saps heat from the oven. If the ground is cold, a fire must be kept burning in the pit to thoroughly warm the ground. If slab-shaped rocks or cobbles are available, they can be used to line the floor and walls of the oven. On beaches, dig high enough that the bottom of the pit is still within dry sand. Sand heats incredibly well and provides the perfect conditions for a ground oven. The pit should be large enough to contain both the food and the cooking rocks.

THE ROCKS AND FIRE

Usually, a ground oven is heated with hot rocks, although when rocks are not available, hard wood embers or lumps broken from termite mounds can be substituted instead. At a Maori *hangi*, I have even seen steel railway tie plates used in the place of rocks.

The rocks chosen are also important: for safety, they need to be dry. Damp or wet rocks may explode when heated. For the same reason, flint and concrete cannot be used as they contain air pockets that will expand when heated, causing the rock to explode or crack. Round, smooth rocks will retain their heat the longest.

Rocks should always be heated slowly; if you place them directly into a hot fire, they are more likely to break. While rocks can be heated in a fire and then placed in the oven pit, the usual method is to place them in a fire constructed in or over the pit. This is the easiest method and burning a fire within the pit provides the advantage of drying and warming the ground, making for a more efficient ground oven.

The fire need not be made with slow-burning hardwood. In fact, a faster-burning fire of smaller wood will be quicker and more convenient. As the fire burns down, the rocks will drop into the pit; to maximise the rocks' heating, try to keep them covered with the fire and embers as the fire burns down to ash.

While the fire is burning, prepare the food for cooking and gather vegetation to use to pack the food in the oven. Large, thick roots can be left whole or cut into smaller pieces and placed in a string bag or light open-weave basket. Game can be quartered. If instead it is cooked whole, hot rocks can be placed inside the ribcage to ensure it cooks throughout. Meat portions should be wrapped in leaves, while fish can be cooked within their own skins.

Once the fire has burned down and the rocks are very hot, remove any remaining pieces of firewood. Distribute the rocks evenly across the pit base. Now lay down a layer of non-toxic green leaves on the rocks. If you want to flavour your food with herbs, place these in as a layer now. Arrange the food atop these with the slower-cooking foods nearest the bottom of the pit and the vegetables in the remaining gaps and the sides. Place another layer of packing vegetation over the top and above this lay another layer of a different vegetation. Broad leaves, such as dock, burdock or butterbur, are ideal.

Next, seal the oven with soil dug out during the excavation of the pit. You will almost certainly need some extra soil for a perfect seal. Once properly sealed, no steam or smoke will be seen to escape from the pit.

Leave the pit to cook. How long? I hear you ask. Now here is the rub: only experience can say. The amount of food, the type of food, the type of rocks, the temperature and many other factors will affect this. My advice is to leave the oven for no less than 1 hour for fish, no less than 2 hours for vegetables and no less than 4 hours for meat, although 6–8 hours is preferable. It is better to overestimate cooking time; nothing is more disappointing than opening the oven to find the food is undercooked.

When preparing to open the oven, have a clean place ready to receive the food packages. Carefully scrape the soil to one side. Take your time to brush as much soil away as possible. Now begin to roll the broad leaves back like rolling up a carpet. Be careful: steam will escape from the pit and will be extremely hot. Rolling back the leaves, if you are careful, will roll away any remaining soil. Now, carefully and allowing the steam to escape ahead of your actions, roll out the top packing vegetation again in the same direction that you rolled away the broad leaves.

Once the steam escapes you will be able to lift out the food packages. Use gloves or tongs as they will be hot. Check that everything, particularly the meat and fish, is cooked. If so, serve and enjoy. Do not touch the rocks: they will still be hot.

DRY GROUND OVEN

The basic ground oven cooks mainly by steaming. It gives more of a roast effect and consequently a different flavour, which suits the cooking of large meat joints, especially a haunch of venison. Personally, I prefer the flavour of the dry oven to the steam pit when cooking meat. This oven does pose the possibility of scorching the meat, however, so practice is necessary.

For this oven, a lined pit works best. Heat the oven and cooking rocks in the usual way (see above). Once they are hot and the fire has burned down, remove the rocks from the pit and brush away any smoking coals. Return three or four rocks.

Oil and season the joint and place it directly atop the rocks. Add more rocks around the meat. Place green sticks over the pit to hold the covering. If possible, use a piece of old canvas over the pit. If not, cover the sticks with packing vegetation and broad leaves, the key point being that this layer does not come into direct contact with the hot rocks. Cover with soil so that the pit is sealed, then leave to cook. When opening the oven, you will need tongs to lift away the hot rocks on top of the joint.

1 Fire heats both the pit and the rocks.

4 The food is protected with a layer of green vegetation and extra hot rocks are placed on top. Green sticks and vegetation are placed over the ground oven to roof it, and then the hole is sealed with soil from the pit.

2 The fire is removed from the pit and the hot rocks placed to pave the pit base.

3 Meat (here, two whole legs of lamb) is placed directly onto the hot rocks and then surrounded by vegetables.

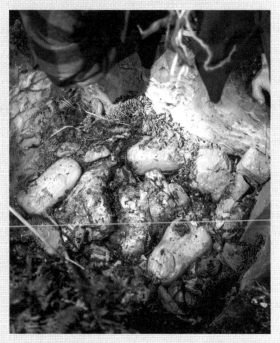

5 Opening the oven, the soil is carefully scraped away and the sealing vegetation rolled back. Wonderful aromas begin to emerge from the pit.

6 The perfectly cooked food is ready to be removed and served.

THE STEAM GROUND OVEN

If I am only cooking large fish, and in quantity, I use a wetter steam pit. This is constructed in the same way as the basic ground oven, with one exception: a straight stick of peeled green wood is placed vertically in the centre of the pit. This must be 2–3cm (1–1½in) in diameter and long enough that it protrudes well above the sealed ground oven.

Heat and fill the oven as described earlier for the basic ground oven, packing the food so that a small gap is left around the vertical stick.

Next, remove the stick by lifting it out vertically. Into the resulting hole, pour 1–2 litres of fresh water and seal the hole over. This ensures a really good steaming throughout the ground oven. I have used this to great effect in the tropics when cooking large marine fish.

THE GROUND OVEN MAT

In many ways, the most difficult part of the ground oven method is finding a suitable covering for the oven. For the smaller ovens this is not necessary as large leaves or a bulk of smaller vegetation will suffice, but for larger ovens, a decent covering makes the difference between food free of soil, or gritty morsels. In the modern world, we can easily secure a sheet of old canvas or hessian, but if you would like to employ a more original method, try weaving a simple mat using straps of willow bark and bundles of grass or soft rush. Well made, a mat like this can last several years.

THE LARGE GROUND OVEN

A large ground oven requires a lot of preparation, the secret of success being many hands making lighter work. The day before the oven will be used, the pit is prepared and lined, the firewood is collected and made ready, and any leaves or string, etc. that will be needed are gathered. Success will require good organisation: I would advise delegating responsibilities. The chef has overall responsibility with trusted assistants supervising the preparation of each component – meat, veg, fruit, etc. Have a timescale in mind: food ready for this time, oven hot by this time, oven sealed at this time, cooking time and dining time.

Very early in the morning, the fire is ignited. While this is burning, other participants are preparing the food: the meat is seasoned and wrapped in leaf packages neatly tied with bark fibre; the vegetables can be sliced to better proportions – peeled and cut potatoes can be contained in an improvised sack of cotton stockingette; fruit needs little preparation for the ground oven – whole bananas, apples and pineapples can be cooked in their skins; even puddings that are normally steamed can be wrapped in cloth and tied with string for the ground oven.

Once ready to cook, green vegetables can be layered over the top of the other ingredients or tucked into spaces.

Once loaded with food, the pit should be spanned with green sticks and a mat cover placed over the top, which is then sealed with soil. The green sticks must be strong enough to withstand the weight of the soil seal. The oven should cook all day so that it is ready for an early evening meal one hour before sunset.

opposite Shelter from the breeze, a good fire and fresh campfire coffee. It is the simplest elements of outdoor cooking that warm the soul.

APPENDIX

INTERNAL COOKING TEMPERATURES

meat	minimum safe	blue	rare	medium rare	medium	medium well	well done
BEEF / VEAL / LAMB							
minced, burgers, meatballs, sausages	71°C 160°F						
whole cuts, steaks, pieces		54°C 129°F	57°C 135°F	63°C 145°F	71°C 160°F	74°C 165°F	77°C 170°F
PORK (ham, pork loin, ribs)							
minced, burgers, meatballs, sausages	71°C 160°F						
whole cuts, steaks, pieces	63°C 145°F	N/A	N/A	63°C 145°F	66°C 150°F	68°C 155°F	71°C 160°F

GAME MEAT	minimum safe
minced, burgers, sausages	74°C 165°F
deer, elk, moose, caribou, reindeer, antelope, pronghorn	74°C 165°F
bear, bison, musk-ox, walrus	74°C 165°F
rabbit, beaver, muskrat	74°C 165°F

GAME BIRDS	minimum safe
whole	82°C 180°F
breasts, roasts	74°C 165°F
thighs, wings	74°C 165°F
stuffing	74°C 165°F

SEAFOOD	minimum safe
fish	70°C 158°F
shellfish	74°C 165°F

POULTRY	minimum safe
minced, burgers, meatballs, sausages	74°C 165°F
pieces, wings, legs, thighs, breasts	74°C 165°F
stuffing	74°C 165°F
whole bird	82°C 180°F

HOT DOGS	minimum safe
hot dogs	74°C 165°F

EGGS	minimum safe
egg dishes	74°C 165°F

BAKING TEMPERATURES

BREAD	temperature
warm water for yeast	41–46°C (106–115°F)
cold water for yeast	15°C (59°F)
bread (lean dough)	88–93°C (190–199°F)
bread (rich dough)	77°C (171°F)
sponge cake	95–98°C (203–209°F)
fruit cake	98–100°C (209–212°F)

right Today, there's no reason not to have a thermometer with you when cooking in a fixed camp. They're the best way to check whether meat is cooked properly.

VEGETABLE STOCK

Fresh vegetable stock is so easy to make and a wonderful base ingredient for a host of dishes. It serves as a vitamin-rich liquid that can be used to cook rice, couscous or quinoa. I prefer to season my sauces, rather than adding salt to the stock.

INGREDIENTS

Makes 2 cups (500ml)

1 onion
2 celery stalks
2 carrots
2–3 garlic cloves, peeled and lightly crushed
sprig of thyme
3 cups (750ml) water

METHOD

1 Peel and chop the onion, and wash and roughly chop the celery and carrots.
2 Put the veg into a deep billycan, then add the garlic and thyme.
3 Cover with cold water and bring to the boil. Simmer for no less than 2 hours.
4 Strain the stock from the vegetables.

VARIATION

Scraps from vegetable preparation can also be added to the stock, such as the cores from peppers, peelings, etc. If you add onion skins to the stock they will darken it, which can be nice for some soups.

MUSHROOM STOCK

Mushroom stock is one of the easiest stocks to make, and is a great way to use leftover trimmings from veg and mushrooms.

INGREDIENTS

Makes 2 cups (500ml)

2 tbsp olive oil
1 onion chopped
2 carrots chopped
1 stick of celery
Alternatively, trimmings from veg
2 sprigs of thyme
1 bay leaf
2 cups chopped mushrooms or mushroom trimmings
1 garlic clove
10 slices of dried mushroom (ideally boletae, but failing this slice and dry common field mushrooms)

METHOD

1 Finely chop the vegetables and fungi.
2 Sweat the veg and mushrooms in the oil over a gentle heat until softened and deeply aromatic. Do not allow to scorch or burn. Keep the lid on.
3 Add the dried mushrooms.
4 Add the bay leaf and the thyme, then cover with water and bring to the boil. Simmer for 45 minutes, with the lid on.
5 Remove the lid and allow the stock to reduce, until it develops the strength of flavour you desire.
6 Strain the stock, squeezing the maximum flavour from the ingredients.

FISH STOCK

I hate to see fish bones wasted in camp. For the sake of a few minutes work, a wonderfully flavoured stock is easy to make and is the perfect base for a fish soup. The secret is to treat this delicate stock with care, never cook it longer than 45 minutes or it will become bitter.

INGREDIENTS

Makes 4 cups (1 litre)

1 onion
2 carrots
2 celery stalks
1 tbsp olive oil
fish bones, heads and scraps
1 cup (250ml) white wine (optional)
water
bouquet garni (see page 43)

METHOD

1 Roughly chop the vegetables, peeling only the onion.
2 Heat the oil in a large billycan, then add the vegetables and sweat for about 15 minutes, until the onion is translucent.
3 Add the fish bits and stir well.
4 Add the wine, if available, then cover everything with cold water and add the bouquet garni.
5 Bring to just below the boil and simmer for 30 minutes but no more than 45 minutes.
6 During the simmering, constantly skim the surface of foam and scum.
7 After cooking, strain out the solids and reserve the stock.

SHELLFISH STOCK

This stock is easy to make even over a hike stove and is a great use of prawn heads or crab shells. Simply delicious: one taste and it will set your culinary imagination on fire to create new recipes. Sometimes wild fennel can be found growing on the coastline and makes a fitting ingredient. If it's not available, use carrots.

INGREDIENTS

Makes 4 cups (1 litre)

1 leek
1 onion
2 celery stalks
1 fennel bulb or 2 carrots
1 tbsp olive oil
crustacean shells
1 cup (250ml) white wine (optional)
water
bouquet garni (see page 43) or other herbs

METHOD

1 Prepare all of the vegetables, chopping them finely. You only need to peel the onion.
2 Heat the oil in a large billycan, add the shells and cook until nicely coloured. Add the chopped vegetables.
3 Sweat the ingredients down until the leek and onion are translucent, then deglaze the pan with wine, if available.
4 Add water to just cover the pan contents, along with a bouquet garni or any herbs you have available.
5 Bring to a high simmer, then cook for no more than 45 minutes over a low flame. Strain the stock.

Cook's tip If you have a fine sieve available or are able to improvise one, the crustacean shells can be crushed with the end of rolling pin-sized stick prior to being added to the pan. This will intensify the flavour, but you do need to be sure you'll be able to completely strain them out at the end or the stock will be gritty.

CHICKEN STOCK

No pre-packaged chicken stock compares to the home-made variety. Stock is so easy to make outdoors where we are cooking over a campfire. Use this stock when making Chicken suprême and taste the difference. I must admit to using more cloves and peppercorns than I have listed below. Experiment and see what you like best.

INGREDIENTS

Makes 4 cups (1 litre)

1 onion
2 carrots
2 celery stalks
chicken carcass and trimmings
1 tbsp olive oil
2 garlic cloves, lightly crushed
1 tsp whole black peppercorns
2 cloves
1 bay leaf
sprig of thyme (optional)
bouquet garni (see page 43)
water

METHOD

1 Peel and dice the onion, and wash and dice the other vegetables.
2 Quarter the chicken carcass.
3 Heat the oil and then cook the chicken carcass until brown, being careful not to let the bones burn.
4 Add the onion, carrot, celery and garlic, black peppercorns and cloves. Sweat until the onion is translucent.

5 Add the bay leaf and the thyme, if using, and the bouquet garni, then cover with water and bring to the boil. Simmer for 2–3 hours or until the flavour is intense. During the simmering, skim away any scum or foam from the surface.
6 Strain the bones out and allow the stock to cool. Remove any fat that solidifies on the surface.

BEEF OR GAME STOCK

Making a dark stock from leftover bones is time-consuming and so really only suited to a fixed camp or cabin situation. However, it makes the best use of ingredients that would otherwise be discarded, is very easy to make and is a delicious ingredient. Incidentally, the marrow fat found on top of the cooled stock is used to make pemmican (a long-lasting ration, made by mixing dried and shredded meat with rendered fat and dried berries, ideal for travel) or carried with dried shredded meat by the First Nations in northern Canada.

INGREDIENTS

Makes 4 cups (1 litre)

1 onion
2 celery stalks
2 carrots
6 tbsp olive oil
meat bones
1 tbsp tomato puree
1 bay leaf
water

METHOD

1 Prepare all of the vegetables, peeling the onion and chopping all of them coarsely.
2 In a large Dutch oven, heat 4 tbsp of the oil, then add the bones to this, along with the tomato puree.
3 Stir the bones to coat in the tomato puree, put the lid on the oven and place over a medium heat. The aim is to cook the bones until they are nicely caramelised and dark brown. They must not be allowed to burn.

4 In a frying pan, heat the remaining 2 tbsp oil and cook the roughly chopped vegetables over a low heat for about 20 minutes, until they are also caramelised.
5 With a cup of water, deglaze the bottom of the Dutch oven, then add the vegetables and their juices to the meat, along with the bay leaf.
6 Add enough cold water to cover the bones by 2cm (1in). Bring to the boil and then leave to simmer for 4–5 hours. During this time, periodically skim away any foam or particles that rise to the surface.
7 Remove the bones with tongs or a slotted spoon and strain the stock.
8 In a cabin or a boat with refrigeration, the stock can be cooled and kept refrigerated for 2–3 days. When cool, remove the fat that rises to the surface. In the absence of refrigeration, the stock should be used immediately.

GRAVY FROM SCRATCH

This is an essential recipe for any wilderness chef. While it will never compare to a gravy made by mining the flavours on the base of a roasting pan, it is not a bad second place. Practise this simple recipe until it becomes second nature. Experiment with adding tiny amounts of redcurrant jelly or honey for sweetening.

INGREDIENTS

Makes 2 cups (500ml)

1 medium onion
1 medium carrot
1 celery stalk
2 tbsp olive oil
½ tbsp balsamic vinegar
2 tbsp plain flour
2 cups (500ml) stock (appropriate to the dish)
2–3 tsp beurre manié (see page 40), or
2 tsp arrowroot or cornflour mixed to a paste with 2 tsp water
salt and ground black pepper, to taste
½ tsp honey (optional)

METHOD

1 Peel the onion and carrot, then finely dice them and the celery stalk.
2 Heat the oil, add the vegetables and sweat down over a low heat for 15–20 minutes, until very soft and beginning to caramelise.
3 Add the balsamic vinegar and cook for a minute, then add the flour and stir to form a roux.
4 Whisk in the stock until smooth, then bring to a simmer and reduce the liquid by about half.
5 Thicken the sauce by adding the beurre manié and whisking it in until smooth and glossy. Alternatively, whisk in the arrowroot or cornflour paste and cook for a couple of minutes.
6 Season to taste. If bitter, sweeten the gravy with a tiny amount of honey.

GRAVY FROM THE PAN

For gravy from the pan, take the cooking pan and use the recipe above, but before adding the flour, use a little water or preferably wine to deglaze the pan, stirring and scraping to incorporate all of the wonderfully flavoured brown residue. Then continue as above.

SIMPLE RED WINE JUS

A simple red wine jus is an elegant accompaniment to a roasted meat dish. It is an extremely quickly made alternative to gravy. A magic trick that is essential for every wilderness chef.

INGREDIENTS

Makes 2 cups (500ml)

1 onion
1 tsp olive oil
2 tsp balsamic vinegar
⅔ cup (175ml) beef stock
 (see page 262)
1½ cups (375ml) stock
1 tbsp butter
salt and ground black
 pepper, to taste

METHOD

1 Peel the onion, then slice it into discs.
2 Heat the oil in a frying pan, then add the onion and fry gently for about 20 minutes, until caramelised.
3 Add the balsamic vinegar and the red wine, reduce until nearly dry, then add the stock.
4 Reduce the jus by half, then finish by adding the butter in small pieces for a glossy finish. Taste and adjust the seasoning as required.

HOLLANDAISE SAUCE

Hollandaise sauce is spectacular but is, I will admit, sometimes a challenge in the windswept outdoor kitchen. But do you aspire to be a wilderness cook or a wilderness chef? Delicacy of touch, boldness, perfect timing and willingness to risk failure – those are the true ingredients of a wilderness hollandaise sauce.

INGREDIENTS

Serves 4

2 tbsp white wine
 vinegar
4 tbsp water
12 lightly crushed
 peppercorns
4 egg yolks
½ cup (125g) butter,
 cut into small chunks
⅗ cup (150ml) hot
 water
juice of ½ lemon
salt and ground black
 pepper, to taste

METHOD

1 In a small pan, heat the vinegar, water and peppercorns and simmer until reduced by half.
2 Whisk in the egg yolks followed by the butter, added a little at a time. Just tickle the pan with enough heat to melt the butter.
3 Whisk in the hot water, add the lemon juice, then season to taste.

BÉARNAISE SAUCE

A challenge for the wilderness chef, this sauce is wonderful with steak, of course, but my favourite way to eat it is to cook a pavé of venison beside the fire (see Robin Hood's Venison Steak on page 71) and use the béarnaise sauce as a sort of dip.

INGREDIENTS

Makes ⅘ cup (200ml)

4 tbsp white wine
   or water
4 tbsp white wine
   vinegar
1 shallot, peeled and
   finely chopped
8 black peppercorns
4 tbsp finely chopped
   tarragon
2 tbsp finely chopped
   chervil (if available)
2 tsp water
2 egg yolks
⅖ cup (100g) hot
   clarified butter
   (see box)
pinch of salt
1 tsp lemon juice

METHOD

1 Put the wine or water, vinegar and shallot in a pan and bring to a simmer.
2 Crush the peppercorns under the flat side of a knife and add them to the pan along with most of the tarragon and chervil – reserve some for the end.
3 Over a low heat, reduce the mixture until it is nearly dry (tilt the pan: there should be 1 tbsp of liquid remaining).
4 Remove the pan from the heat and allow the mixture to cool.
5 Meanwhile, clarify the butter by melting and spooning away any solid matter from the surface.

6 Add the 2 tsp of water to the herb reduction and whisk in the egg yolks. Tease the pan over the lowest heat and keep whisking: the aim is to emulsify the eggs in the sauce and not to allow them to scramble. This will take a considerable amount of whisking.
7 When the mixture thickens to the consistency of very smooth thick cream, remove it from the heat.
8 Now one spoonful at a time, whisk in the warm clarified butter, adding a pinch of salt as you go.
9 Finally, mix in a good squeeze of lemon juice and the reserved chopped herbs.

PALOISE

This is identical to béarnaise sauce except that it includes mint instead of tarragon. It is a brilliant accompaniment to lamb chops cooked on the griddle.

CLARIFIED BUTTER

Melt some unsalted butter in a pan or frying pan over a low heat, then spoon away the foam and solid particles until a clear liquid is left behind.

TOMATO SAUCE

A tomato sauce is another classic chef speciality. A simple way to transform so many dishes from meat cooked on skewers to impromptu pasta. This sauce has more than once saved the day when a wilderness kitchen intervention has been required.

INGREDIENTS

Makes 4 cups (1 litre)

2 carrots
1 onion
2–3 bacon rashers
1 tbsp butter
1 tbsp flour
2 tbsp tomato puree
4 cups (1 litre) vegetable or chicken stock (see pages 259 and 261)
2 x 400g (15oz) cans chopped tomatoes
2 garlic cloves, peeled and crushed
2 shallots, peeled and finely chopped
bouquet garni (see page 43)
salt and ground black pepper, to taste
knob of butter, to finish (optional)

METHOD

1 Peel and dice the carrots and onion and roughly dice the bacon.
2 Melt the butter in a large pan or billycan over a medium heat, then add the bacon and fry for a few minutes, until just cooked.
3 Add the carrots and onion and sweat for about 15 minutes, until softened.
4 Add the flour and mix to form a roux. Cook for about 2 minutes, until lightly golden.
5 Add the tomato puree and cook for 2–3 minutes, stirring.
6 Remove the roux to a bowl and leave it to cool.

7 Heat the stock in a separate pan until boiling.
8 Wipe the roux pan clean, then replace the cold roux and place over a medium heat. Add a couple of cups of the boiling stock and whisk until smooth, then add the remaining stock and whisk until lump-free.
9 Add the chopped tomatoes, garlic, shallots and bouquet garni. Put the lid on the pan or billycan and simmer for 1 hour.
10 Season to taste, then strain to remove the solid ingredients. Classically, the sauce is finished with a knob of butter, but this is optional.

REAL VANILLA CUSTARD

It is possible to use canned or packet custard – frankly, no one is going to complain – but, equally frankly, real custard is easy to prepare and is matchless. Fresh vanilla pods are easily included in a camp larder and are simply one of nature's greatest flavour marvels. Cream can be the canned variety or, if camping in less wild circumstances, a good excuse for a hike to a dairy.

INGREDIENTS

Makes 2 cups (500ml)

6 egg yolks
2 tsp cornflour
3 tbsp caster sugar
2 cups (500ml) double cream
2 vanilla pods

METHOD

1 Put the egg yolks, cornflour and sugar in a medium billycan and whisk together until smooth.

2 Place the cream in a small billycan.

3 Split open the vanilla pods and scrape out the seeds with the back of a knife. Add the vanilla seeds and the empty pods to the cream.

4 Heat very gently until just below a simmer, then remove from the heat and allow to stand for a couple of minutes for the aroma of the vanilla to flavour the cream.

5 Fish out the pods and pour the warm cream slowly into the egg mixture while whisking continuously.

6 Place the custard over a very gentle heat and continue whisking until it thickens. Go carefully or you will overcook it and it will become lumpy.

7 Once cooked, it can be served immediately.

Cook's tip
If you overcook the custard, remove it from the heat and immediately transfer to a fresh billycan and whisk until smooth.

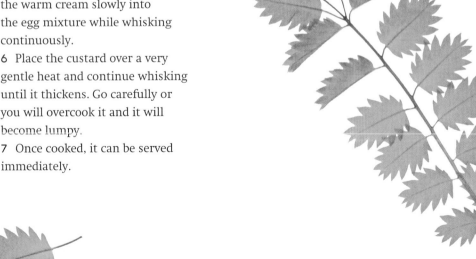

INDEX

ACKNOWLEDGEMENTS

When I started on this book, I had no idea what fun it would be, nor how demanding. Outdoor cooking is in many cases an instinctive process without easy measurement of quantities, temperatures and timings: you learn as you cook. So, the first challenge was to establish quantities for recipes which I most often quantify intuitively by experience and by taste. The second challenge was having to both cook the dishes outdoors in the vagaries of the British climate and to photograph them, perhaps the ideal training for plate spinning. Despite all of this the whole process was also tremendous fun, the result of the wonderful support I received from my family, friends and colleagues. Fortunately, mentioning no names, there was only one occasion when a dish was eaten before I could photograph it. To all who offered their help I offer my deepest thanks.

Particular thanks must go to the following:

My mother, who throughout my childhood was a wonderful cook and whose skill first inspired me to take an interest in cooking, ingredients and techniques.

My darling wife Ruth for her constant love, support and encouragement. Her willing assistance in the field was invaluable.

The late Dr Derek Reid, and Gillian Wynn-Ruffhead, who taught me to identify and to love wild fungi. Learning to cook with wild fungi was the single most important spark to the flame beneath my pan.

My agent Jackie Gill, for handling the commercial aspects of the project so ably.

Elizabeth Multon and Kathryn Beer at Bloomsbury for holding their nerve with the recipe that is the book itself.

Jo Lee, for providing sage advice regarding oriental cooking and sharing her recipe for Rendang curry.

Andrew and Kate Morton for providing access to woodland in which to cook and photograph many of the dishes.

James and Karen Baird for access to the beach and wild fennel.

My dearest friend Edward Cadogan for allowing me to poach one of his brown trout and Chanterelles in Scotland.

Glen Burrows, Hugh Johnson and David Southey for their assistance in the photography.

Steve Gurney and the Woodlore team for their constant support.

All of the many Woodloreans, who over the past 36 years of field courses and expeditions have suggested I write this book.

Finally, and importantly, the many first nation cooks beside whose fires I have learned to cook without utensils and ingredients and who keep alive the flame of humanity's most original kitchen.

To you all...

Bon Appetit

PICTURE CREDITS